Classical Music, Why Bother?

Hearing the World of Contemporary Culture through a Composer's Ears

JOSHUA FINEBERG
Harvard University

Routledge
Taylor & Francis Group
New York   London

Routledge is an imprint of the
Taylor & Francis Group, an informa business

Published in 2006 by
Routledge
Taylor & Francis Group
270 Madison Avenue
New York, NY 10016

Published in Great Britain by
Routledge
Taylor & Francis Group
2 Park Square
Milton Park, Abingdon
Oxon OX14 4RN

Printed in the United States of America on acid-free paper
10 9 8 7 6 5 4 3 2 1

International Standard Book Number-10: 0-415-97173-X (Hardcover)
International Standard Book Number-13: 978-0-415-97173-7 (Hardcover)
Library of Congress Card Number 2005033461

Library of Congress Cataloging-in-Publication Data

Fineberg, Joshua.
    Classical music, why bother? : hearing the world of contemporary culture through a composer's ears / Joshua Fineberg.
        p. cm.
    Includes bibliographical references (p.) and index.
    ISBN 0-415-97173-X (hb : alk. paper) -- ISBN 0-415-97174-8 (pb : alk. paper) 1.
    Music--Philosophy and aesthetics. 2. Music--Social aspects. I. Title.

ML3800.F444 2006
781.6'8--dc22   2005033461

Taylor & Francis Group
is the Academic Division of Informa plc.

Visit the Taylor & Francis Web site at
http://www.taylorandfrancis.com

and the Routledge Web site at
http://www.routledge-ny.com

CONTENTS

Acknowledgments

The ideas in this book have been shaped over many years of casual and not so casual discussions with countless people I have encountered. Most essential, though, have been my interactions with the students passing through my undergraduate courses since I began teaching at Harvard in 2000. My discussions with them have helped me to see the absolute necessity of engaging with a broader public, if my profession is to survive.

Leonard Bernstein famously quipped that in his day the professors of Harvard's music department believed that music was meant to be seen and not heard; my experience, however, has been completely different. The music department is one of the very few places I know where music is both carefully seen and deeply heard. Art music is taken very seriously as both something to do and something to study, offering an ideal environment for a practitioner like me to engage with some of the world's finest scholars and students. Moreover, the Walton/Harvard Fellowship, awarded by the music department and the Fromm Foundation in collaboration with the William Walton Foundation, allowed me to have a concentrated chunk of time within Lady Susana Walton's idyllic gardens at La Mortella to do the heavy lifting of turning a moderate-length article into the start of this book. Lady Walton deserves special thanks for putting up with what I am sure must have been the horribly boring dinner-table rehearsal of several of the book's central arguments.

While I cannot individually thank everyone who has contributed to this book, particular thanks must go to three people. First, Andrew O'Hehir, the arts editor for the webzine *Salon.com*, gave me invaluable help and advice for the article "Classical Music, Why Bother?" which *Salon.com* first published in October 2002; many parts of the text in the first three chapters originally appeared in that article. My father also deserves special thanks: He has tried throughout my life to teach me how to write prose and, as if that Sisyphean task were not enough, was also willing to put up with my stubbornness and petulance through several drafts of this manuscript. Finally and most importantly, my wife, Ioana, has had to bear with me throughout the whole process, arguing out each idea in turn, and was forced to endure my accepting yet another project on top of everything else.

PRELUDE

Even among members of the supposed "educated elite," questions concerning the nature and purpose of art no longer have the clear answers that they might have had in the past. This, I believe, is the underlying cause of the rupture between contemporary art music and its audience that has grown of late to Grand Canyon-like proportions. I hope this book will offer my perspective, that of a working professional composer of contemporary "Western art music," regarding these questions and the long-term impact our society's answers to them will have on future art. My perspective may seem far too specialized at a time when many people probably don't know that "classical" composers still exist and the culture at large dictates that most of those who do either don't care or resent our intrusion and demands. However, we happen to be among a small handful of groups in society who are so directly affected by these seeming abstractions that we cannot avoid confronting them.

I am not a philosopher or a cultural critic; I am a composer and teacher of music. Over the last dozen years, I have studied, worked, and taught in Paris, New York, and now Cambridge, Massachusetts. In all these places I have listened to and participated in innumerable (and virtually indistinguishable) conversations that touch upon the nature and purpose of art in our society without addressing them directly. Few of these discussions move past a very short-term view of some immediate problem regarding art and its reception. We may discuss how to fill the hall for a particular event; who the really "great" living composers are; why can't we sell more copies of some CD; what's a real modern masterpiece; or any of a host of other momentarily important issues. It is very hard, however, to believe that this or that decision or tactic will really affect the fundamental trends in the world of so-called "art music." Over more than fifty years, this music has moved towards an increasingly marginal social and commercial existence, an ever more historically oriented repertoire, and an older and older audience; moreover, these trends show no signs of meaningfully improving.

During the last few years, a significant portion of my teaching has been directed at students who are not music majors. Through my discussions with this highly educated, but non-musically oriented, group of students, I have come to feel that ideas concerning the nature and purpose of art were no longer givens. Working with this more heterogeneous set of students, I became increasingly convinced of the need to address to a nonspecialist public some thoughts on the role of art in society, especially difficult art (and its relationship to the lack of audience for contemporary music).

I hope to address in a personal, rather than a detached philosophical, way some of the greatest of all abstractions: art, culture, society, worth, ethics, and meaning. Yet rather than jumping right into these rather daunting issues, I propose to begin by recounting a conversation I have had again and again with different people at various receptions, dinners, cocktail parties, student meetings, and lunches. It is not so much a real introduction as it is a way of setting the tone for what is to follow — please think of it as a sort of prelude.

The discussion often begins like this: "So, you're a composer?" (A guffaw or an incredulously raised eyebrow is optional.)

As I answer this in the affirmative, I'm not quite sure which path the conversation will take, but I am sure it will be well trod. The next question is often about my music: perhaps, "So, what kind of music do you write?" or "What sort of songs do you compose?"

While there is nothing at all wrong with the question in principle, in practice there is almost never a meaningful way to answer it. Let me explain by using an analogy: I am color-blind, and when people find that out, their first question is usually, "So, when you look at this [they hold up a random object], what color do you see?" I then try to explain that I can't say what I see. We have no shared vocabulary; I've never seen green or blue as a person with normal color vision would see it. I explain that to the extent that I am capable of figuring out what label most people think should go with a given object I can answer, but I know that even if we reach agreement on the label, it still does not mean that we see the same thing in the same way (since my retinal cones are defective, due to a fairly common inherited trait).

When it comes to music, we also lack a shared vocabulary; in this case, however, it is not due to an inequality of perceptual capacities. On the contrary — we hear essentially the same thing but lack a shared context. Therefore, I generally feel impelled to attempt an answer, even though I am skeptical that any verbal answer could really be helpful. In good faith, someone with little or no exposure to contemporary music is asking me to conjure the sonic image of something completely unfamiliar using a few words. (Try describing one of Mark Rothko's large color field paintings to someone who has never seen an abstract painting of any kind, without reducing the description to something equally applicable to a multicolor stone-washed T-shirt.) I usually try to answer in a way that will help my questioner categorize what I do, rather than actually undertake the difficult (and, I suspect, not usually desired) challenge of evoking a sonic image, which a complete answer to his question would require.

First, I explain that my music is "classical." By that, I mean that it is written for mostly the same instruments and ensembles, and using essentially the same notational system, as what they think of as classical music (Bach, Mozart, Beethoven, Brahms, etc.). While many caveats would be necessary to make that last statement completely accurate, I usually leave it at that and go on. I explain that while I and other composers of contemporary classical music feel that our work is the continuation of the classical tradition, it often does not sound at all like that music. I continue by saying that it often sounds quite different from popular or film music as well. By this point both the questioner and I may well be growing frustrated at the difficulty of communicating with such a limited body of common terms. Therefore, I try to mention a few names of composers just in case the listener has chanced upon something that might give us a point of departure. I mention some of the most celebrated composers of contemporary classical music (Boulez, Ligeti, Berio, Grisey, Stockhausen, etc.).

Often, none of the names are even vaguely familiar to the individual, or he or she shows the sort of disembodied recognition that comes from having seen a name in print or heard it in a discussion (e.g., "Boulez — didn't he conduct the New York Philharmonic?"). It is one of the truly unfortunate consequences of contemporary music's marginalization that, through no fault of their own, even highly cultured individuals — who would be embarrassed not to have read a book by a well-known author or seen an important art exhibition — have no knowledge whatsoever of these composers' work. This kind of music has been pushed so far outside of the cultural mainstream that hardly anyone would feel the slightest compunction about failing to recognize the names of the most important contemporary composers.

Classical composers have become the equivalent of some nearly extinct species of European men from the eighteenth and nineteenth centuries whose modern-day descendants, if they exist in some lost corner of a swamp, have long ceased to affect mainstream cultural consciousness. Why would anyone keep track of the most renowned steelsmiths making samurai swords? While this was an important and respected art in feudal Japan, such activities are totally irrelevant today except for souvenir collectors. I suspect that, for many, contemporary music of the sort I practice has no more cultural relevance than the work of those few artisans still practicing ancient techniques for forging steel. Yet, here my poor partner in this conversation is face to face with a living composer.

At some point we give up our blind attempts to name the elephant by fondling its parts and start dancing around the really big questions, the ones they really want to ask.

The first big question for all of us, whether we're four or forty-four, is always "Why?"

Usually people are too polite to spit out that word, but they must be thinking it: "Why?" "Why would a grown man do such an obscure, irrelevant thing? After all, I didn't even really think there still *were* composers." Being a rock star or a concert pianist might be a crazy ambition, but that is because the chance of success is so slim. Being a contemporary composer — having to compete with the giants of the last 300 years in an environment where even the most successful are hardly known and make modest incomes — why dedicate a life to that? It seems absolutely crazy.

If recruiting for today's classical music composers were done in the want ads, I'm sure nobody in his or her right mind would sign up. Can you imagine the text of the ad?

> WANTED: Contemporary classical music composers. Preparation should ideally begin before age seven. At least fifteen years of eye-straining, back-breaking, unpaid, or even costly efforts will eventually be met, at best, with hostility or, more likely, with indifference. Financial prospects vary from nonexistent (or in many cases negative) to mediocre. Only one out of several thousand applicants need even dream of a subsistence income from his music. The only potential for a secure but limited income is that a very small percentage of applicants may be offered the chance to instruct future prospects in a structure quite similar to a pyramid scheme.

With other musicians or with regular concertgoers, the conversation often takes another tack. These are people whose love of music (at least older music) is such that they don't wonder why. The question they really want to ask is closer to "How?" "How can you hope to make a meaningful addition to an impossibly exalted corpus?" A more typical phrasing might be something like this: "Do you really believe that any recent music can truly equal the works of _____ [fill in the blank with whichever timeless genius you prefer: Bach, Mahler, Mozart, Brahms, etc.]?"

In some ways, the "how" question is easier to address than the "why." As you will no doubt have already surmised, I do believe that wonderfully great music is still being written and that even in our modern society it is important enough to dedicate a life to; however, any answer I propose will probably fail to satisfy the questioner. No matter how passionately I might argue for the potential greatness of new works, my opponent is likely to remain unconvinced. Even if he — or she — wants to accept what I say, he cannot because of the next question: "Where?" "Where is the audience?" If I'm right that there is all this amazing music out there, then where is the audience that ought to have been won over by now?

This is perhaps the question that musicians and critics think about most when discussing or writing about contemporary music. Anyone who reads the arts section of *The New York Times* or *The New Yorker* will have read countless think pieces about why contemporary music is not more popular. These ruminations often fall into several broad categories:

1. Some are written by composers who blame the audiences for not making the personal investment necessary to understand their art.

2. Some come from critics who bemoan the inaccessibility of the work of today's composers.

3. Sometimes a critic will laud one or another newly arrived "revolutionary" composer (often his or her personal discovery). Unfortunately, this revolution usually consists of using the classical instrumentarium to produce works that sound like pale imitations of popular music, or being radical enough to write music that sounds like something a particularly hopeless student of Brahms might have come up with (pandering is considered both positive and progressive in this context; it is like lauding as revolutionary a sex therapist who advocates rediscovering the missionary position).

4. Some "more serious" critics write pieces beseeching listeners to make the personal investment that the composers (mentioned in point number one) berated these same listeners for not having made up until now.

5. Some pieces offer no hope; they are darkly pessimistic, mourning the dismal future of classical music (usually citing poor demographics for season ticket holders or donations at major musical organizations.)

6. Some pieces attempt to offer a triumphal solution, hailing some organization or composers' marketing efforts that seem, at least temporarily, to have successfully hoodwinked some sought-after market segment (young concertgoers, for example) into attending a concert or opera. The really sad versions of this story are when we learn that the ever-diminishing resources dedicated to cul-

ture have been used to support a multimillionaire rock star performing pop tunes with orchestral accompaniment in a so-called
effort to reach new audiences (perhaps this sort of outreach is
effective in winning some orchestra patrons over to pop music).

7. A final sort of piece falls back on the ever-present human interest profile. This sort of story is, I suppose, meant to convince us
that if composers are hardworking or likable, hating the music is
somehow petty.

In my imagined conversation, I won't offer arguments that correspond to any of these models — though in the heat of the moment I
have sometimes fallen back on one of those golden oldies. In this book,
I wish us to look at all three of these problems (Why, How, Where)
differently. No standard argument is sufficient, or there would be no
need to continue discussing these questions. I believe that the real
issues at hand are not purely musical and, therefore, no stylistic discussions — no matter how intellectually probing or unabashedly populist
— would address them. I'm convinced that the real reason you see or
hear less and less classical music of any kind and hardly any new music
on your TV or radio is related to the changing place accorded to art in
general within contemporary society.

In the current era, when the *Rite of Spring* has already outlived all but
the oldest audience members (who still think of it as a bit risqué), we
cannot address either the reason that composers are drawn to writing
contemporary classical music or the audience's rejection of (or, worse,
indifference to) contemporary works without confronting the "A word"
(Art) head-on. To go beyond a quick, placating answer to something
with real relevance, we will have to enlarge the subject to art and its
place in society. I'm afraid that I'm going to have to be a bit of a bore,
that guy with whom you may come to regret beginning a conversation.
I'm really going to try to answer those three very important questions
even if the answer takes us far afield and forces me to monopolize the
conversation. Moreover, I'm not going to give you my cocktail party
response; instead, I'll try my best to answer these questions in the rest
of this book. If you aren't up for the ride, now is the time to look at
your watch, mumble some lame excuse about forgetting you had an
appointment, and head for the door.

By playing the blame game — did composers drive away the audience, or has the audience abandoned its responsibilities? — we have ignored a fundamental difference between what composers think they are offering and what audiences think they are, or should be, receiving. Most composers, since at least the nineteenth century, have held a deeply felt, quasi-religious belief in "Art"; I know that I certainly do. This is, I think, what leads us to choose the profession in spite of the unpleasantly poor hourly wage that it brings most of us. We believe that if through determination, hard work, and talent we are able to make truly great works of art, sooner or later people will grapple with these works, come to see their value, and develop the sense of awe we feel in the presence of true masterpieces. This is not to say that many composers are certain that they themselves are writing masterpieces. It has more to do with a belief in the possibility of masterworks and the inevitability that these works, once extant, will eventually receive recognition. Ultimately, we believe that great art enriches the world whether or not the world knows or cares.

An analogy that comes to mind for the situation faced by contemporary classical musicians is the environmental movement. For years discussions about species extinction (at least those that reached the general public) centered on specific abuses: stopping poachers, eliminating a pesticide, saving a nesting ground. The real problem, though, is more systemic: the ever-shrinking size of the habitat and the increasing competition with humans for a share of finite resources.

I think that something parallel needs to happen if we are to understand the situation in the arts. There is not a single cause, whether on the part of audience or composer, but a changing environment to which the kind of art and music that has thrived for hundreds of years in the West may no longer be well adapted. Changes in our society are having profound effects on the artistic ecosystem that has allowed nonfunctional, nonpopular art to be valued and supported (at least enough for it to have come into existence). Although we as a society may ultimately decide that this kind of music is out of date and built on superseded, elitist premises, I believe we should at least pause and reflect on what we stand to lose if we decide no longer to support and foster the work of today's classical music composers. We must at least take note of these changes or we may find very soon that things we believed would always flourish have mysteriously gone extinct, leaving us with a very different silent spring than the one that was averted by banning DDT. In other words, this is perhaps my one and only chance to present you with my best case for why I believe what I do is important and necessary, and why I think you should care that it might disappear.

1

AESTHETIC VALUE

It is now taken for granted that nothing which concerns art can be taken for granted any more: neither art itself, nor art in its relationship to the whole, nor even the right of art to exist.

— Theodor W. Adorno

"Wait one second," you say. "Art is not so imperiled as all that." You might be thinking something along the same lines as Alice Goldfarb Marquis, an independent scholar who works in various fields as a sort of arts journalist and cultural critic. She likes to take the contrarian's perspective that what the arts need is less government support (*not* more), therefore she regularly shows up on panel discussions about arts subsidies; in a "crossfire" world people who take an opposing view are always precious, even if the debates are sponsored by subsidized organizations. At the conclusion of *Art Lessons: Learning from the Rise and Fall of Public Funding*, her rather damning critique of well-meant but, she believes, ultimately misguided arts funding in the late-twentieth century, Dr. Marquis asserts that the National Endowment for the Arts is a group that "purveys a multitude of fictions: [...] that non-profit arts deserve support while commercial arts do not; that there exists a distinct cultural realm worthy of subsidy, a realm easily distinguished from simple entertainment; and worst of all that the arts in America would perish without federal intervention."[1]

Like Dr. Marquis, you are probably thinking that we have had painting since at least the cave paintings in Lascaux and Chauvet (ca. 25,000 years ago); and it appears that even the Neanderthals made music with tuned bone flutes. Indeed, even in my worst fits of alarmism, I do not claim that music and the visual arts are in any danger of disappearing from the world. But Adorno meant something slightly more, or different, than that when he referred to "art."

One of the fictions Marquis feels the NEA purveys is the existence of a "cultural realm worthy of subsidy, a realm easily distinguished from simple entertainment." And it is this particular realm, fictional though it may be, that I fear is in danger of disappearing. I believe the passage of this realm out of our world would be tragic — even for the vast majority of people who have no interest in art that is made there.

Dr. Marquis believes that the arts in America have declined from what she perceived to be a high point in the twenty years after World War II toward ever-lower depths. She blames this decline on the cumulative effects of a centralized bureaucratic source of government arts support (the NEA) and, more generally, of the nonprofit structure of arts organizations and universities in America. She believes that these kinds of institutions inevitably reward mediocrity. By focusing only on America and only on the second half of the twentieth century, she can ignore the defects of earlier funding schemes — used by assorted states, princes, kings, and popes — that nonetheless produced art she would have more trouble summarily dismissing. She can blame ineffective bureaucracies and conservatism, as if these were new problems. All of her sociological and economic data do show changes in the acceptance and importance of subsidized art, but I think they are not the changes she believes them to be. There has been a slow shift in worldview over the last hundred years or so that has accelerated in the last thirty years. This change is as far-reaching in its own way as the Copernican revolution. Fifty years ago the cultural realm that Marquis mocks would still, in fact, have been worthy of subsidy, not because the

NEA said so and not because it was easily distinguishable from simple entertainment, but because it was better: The art produced within this realm had more worth, or so the public and government believed. (I do not intend to imply that it was therefore easier to get funding — people's attachment to their money has not changed — only that the premise behind subsidizing art was widely accepted even though this art was no more popular in absolute terms at that time.)

The psychologist Nicholas Humphrey wrote a book debunking claims of paranormal activity, called *Leaps of Faith*,[2] in which he quite persuasively argues that, in spite of all their surface differences, all religions (and more broadly all belief in the supernatural) are at least tacitly dependent on a dualist view of existence. Belief in afterlives, reincarnations, miracles, divinities, and so on, all fundamentally depend on a more basic belief in an immaterial soul — or at least in the existence of a nonphysical, nonmaterial realm. Likewise, a true belief in art is also predicated on an underlying conceptual framework that depends just as absolutely on a belief in abstract criteria of worth. This notion, which is profoundly out of fashion today, has formed the underpinning of artistic endeavor in the West for a very long time. Adherents of this idea believe that even if societal fashions or institutional structures are opposed to a particular artist or work, some essential greatness (or lack thereof) will ultimately determine the worth of the art object if given the chance. And even if the work is never recognized, it is still of equal (albeit latent) value. In other words, a Rembrandt hanging in the woods would still be great even if no one had the good fortune to see it. Partisans in the "culture wars" tried to attack these notions, but that battle mixed the issue of what should be in the canon with whether there should be a canon at all. Moreover, it constantly mixed artistic values and political ones in a way that eliminates the possibility of really discussing art.

Contrary to most contemporary ways of thinking, I believe that taste and social constructions are of decidedly secondary importance if there is such a thing as intrinsic value or worth. Composers often speak of pieces being well constructed or clever, even sometimes brilliant — and then say that they don't particularly care for them. This is because they see personal preference as being much less important and enduring than these other, harder to define criteria of worth. This should not be an unfamiliar concept, because it is for this very reason that even real Shakespeare haters are unlikely to criticize the quality of his verse. We can all feel the genius even if we are not all sensitive to the charms (at least this is what I tell myself).

Some composers have no doubt begun to bristle by this point, thinking that they are not so cavalier as to completely disregard public taste and societal demand. And though they may even believe this, ultimately they are wrong. If taste and society were the real yardstick, then the *Billboard* Hot 100 would be the true arbiter of worth and value (in the noneconomic sense, as it already is in the economic sense) and any "classical" composer holding that view is in the wrong business. This is not to say (as some have done) that success is a reflection of *low* cultural value: It is merely to say that the worth of a work is ultimately either intrinsic to it (as I believe) and therefore completely independent of success or a lack thereof, or it is determined by societal reception — in which case the most flash-in-the-pan "boy band" is "better" than just about any "classical" composer. From this point of view, while an individual composer may feel he is considering both his audience and posterity, the work will ultimately be valued either solely on its intrinsic merits (if there are such things) or solely on the reception it receives. Whether high ideals or low commerce motivated the work is ultimately irrelevant; the value or reception of the work will be what counts, not the creator's intentions or motivations.

Moreover, if you believe that something like intrinsic value exists, then the outreach efforts many arts organizations make seem quite puzzling. If the cost of reaching people is to destroy or at least dilute the "value" of what you are offering, then there is no gain to be had. Arts organizations are being subsidized to promote fine art, not mediocre entertainment. We must not forget that each ticket sold, each show repeated, is usually a financial loss, not a gain — even when the tickets are as expensive as seats at the Metropolitan Opera. The only possible (and therefore mandatory) gain achieved by subsidized art is cultural, not economic.

You may think there ought to be a middle way; things would certainly be easier for all of us if there were. Could we not somehow evaluate quality, accessibility, and popularity in some sort of astutely weighted equation that would make everyone happy? After many years of trying, however, I have never come up with a middle ground that does not sit on a very slippery slope. Every attempt to construct an intermediate framework seems rapidly to devolve into one of two opposing world-views: Any system for evaluating works ultimately depends on either public reception or an attempted assessment of the works' "intrinsic" merits. Ad hoc systems of this kind justify particular actions but don't address the underlying trends.

Some might object to my emphasis on this dichotomy, but our society has reached a junction where making a choice has become inevitable. To return to our analogy regarding the immaterial soul, one can claim to believe in a basically materialistic worldview and yet hope for an aphysical eternal afterlife; this is the essence of Pascal's wager. (Pascal's wager is the calculation that if there is no God there are no negative consequences from falsely believing in one; while if there is a God the price for disbelief is eternal damnation. Thus Pascal asserts that belief is by far the safer bet.) But times occur when one's life is truly in the balance, a choice between flesh and spirit is unavoidable, and neither option is without consequence. (I think this is why some creationists fight so hard against all forms of scientific proof: They realize that ultimately materialism and an immaterial soul cannot coexist.) Facing up to this dichotomous choice is not something most of us like to do.

We live in a deeply inconsistent society, where reliance on science and rationality is much greater (or at least widespread) than at any time in the past, yet large numbers of people still manage to believe in UFOs and government conspiracies conducted with perfect secrecy — not to mention the widespread religious fervor in contemporary America that rivals that of the Medieval era. Current debate about whether Intelligent Design is a rival to evolution that belongs in school or simply a religious fairy tale is only one instance where we will be forced to make a choice that will inevitably seem entirely unacceptable to a large group of people on the other side of the divide. Although humans are very good individually at *not* reconciling our incompatible beliefs, society ultimately makes choices and sets priorities, even if we don't realize it until many years later. In the domain of subsidized arts, I believe that we have reached such a decision point.

Let's back up a bit and look at what brought us here. It may well be that this crisis in belief, this elimination of hierarchies of value from our worldview, goes back to the secularization of culture that has proceeded since the Enlightenment. In speaking about cultural modernity, Jürgen Habermas recalls the following idea from Max Weber:

> He characterized cultural modernity as the separation of the substantive reason expressed in religion and metaphysics into three autonomous spheres. They are: science, morality and art. These came to be differentiated because the unified world-views of religion and metaphysics fell apart. Since the 18th century, the problems inherited from these older world-views could be arranged so as to fall under specific aspects of validity: truth, normative rightness, authenticity and beauty. Scientific discourse, theories of morality, jurisprudence and the production and criticism of art could in turn be institutionalized. Each domain of culture could be made to correspond to culture professions in which problems could be dealt with as the concerns of special experts.[3]

This system could work throughout the late eighteenth, nineteenth, and early twentieth centuries because we were willing to accept its premise that "truth, normative rightness, authenticity and beauty" all existed; moreover, we were willing to believe that they could be evaluated and if not determined in absolute terms, at least they could be arranged hierarchically (e.g., this new theory is more true than the old one; because we can only add one more painting to this room we will take this one because it is more beautiful or more important). By the mid-twentieth century, thinkers like Thomas Kuhn were questioning this premise even with regard to truth. Kuhn believed that because some aspects of older theories might be more valid than some (usually peripheral) aspects of newer theories, it was unfair to think of the new theory as more "true." Kuhn believed we should simply see these new ideas as a different "paradigm."[4] He felt that any sort of hierarchy was an illusion. He did not, however, take this further and suggest how one might proceed if we were to accept his ideas. Must we teach phlogiston theory along with everything else? If we cannot judge the validity of one idea over another, I think NASA is in for many more disappointing and costly failures in the future.

A belief in intrinsic values that can be evaluated has shaped our entire system of cultural production and delivery over several centuries. Museum curators, artistic directors, ministers of culture, music directors, and all sorts of nabobs from the chattering class were there to sift through the masses of mediocre work and find those with real quality. They were Habermas's "special experts," and to get their positions they had to demonstrate the acuity of their judgment, at least in principle. With each choice they were to some extent placing their career on the line. A poor judgment reflected even more on them than on the artist who made the work, because they were the person who was supposed to know better. This was almost the inverse of the current pop music or market-oriented system, where music is played for demographically sorted focus groups, and — presuming the sampling techniques are adequate — it's immediately obvious what's a hit and what's a flop.

Over the last few decades, even the most revered cultural institutions have been affected by "market-think." You need to have a clear theme or a marquee name: something to pull in the customer. But because even hit shows lose money, you also need to convince advertisers to be "sponsors." Most major symphonies are giving marketing directors the equivalent of veto power over the music directors. If you look at covers of recent recordings by classical soloists you will be amazed at the amount of cheesecake or beefcake that goes into marketing. The fine young violinist Hilary Hahn has a Web site (http://www.hilaryhahn.com) that looks as though it should be the publicity site for a new show on the WB about a beautiful teen violinist and her struggle to balance being a teenager with the rigors of art and touring. (I want credit if they actually launch that series.) In 2004 *The New York Times* published a piece about how difficult it was for another attractive young violinist to be taken seriously after posing nude (with a carefully positioned violin) on her first album cover. She seemed to feel it especially unfair to judge her in this manner because her taste in music is so conservative. (God forbid we get beautiful, naked, contemporary music performers!) When you look at those photos and the seasons now offered by classical music institutions you have to wonder: Are they listening for the next great composition or performer who will transform how we hear, or are they instead looking for a cute girl or a sexy guy or a performer who wears strapless gowns or has an attitude, in an effort to repackage what they think is a recipe that works?

This is all over the cultural world. Does anyone believe that the Guggenheim exhibits on motorcycles or Armani suits are driven solely by their artistic merit and not the needs of sponsorship and patronage (read: advertising). Moreover, if they are merely being held to attract a "larger" public, what is the point when each ticket is sold at a loss anyhow?

One of the books I came across while doing research for this volume was Alvin Reiss's *Don't Just Applaud — Send Money!*[5] This volume presents 139 pages of gadgets and gimmicks used by real arts groups to trick or at least prod people into supporting their causes. It contains no advice about the quality of art or really trying to help people grapple with what you are offering; it only offers stories of fund-raising successes, like the very successful effort of the Kamloops Art Gallery in Canada, which bought 1,500 ceramic cows, put them on display in a grass field, and then resold them to donors for twice what they paid. This was apparently so successful that the art gallery still stocks and resells (presumably at a profit) these ceramic cows. Other suggestions for how to help the arts in America included sending out joke-filled postcards soliciting donations. Another category of ideas included suggestions for how to completely reshape your programs to supposedly attract a public. The Long Wharf Theatre in New Haven brought in Julia Child to give a cooking demonstration — so perhaps The Food Channel is the real future of the arts. I think the blurb on the back cover sums up the strange attitude we often confront in the arts. Jane Alexander, then chairman of the NEA, says: "The bottom line he [Reiss] illuminates is this: Be as creative in your marketing and fundraising as you are at your art." With that as her attitude is it any surprise that, tiny though the NEA's budget is, as of 1991 it managed to spend more than half (53 percent) on administration, grants panels, and "infrastructure."[6] After all, I'm sure the NEA feels that its administrative work is just as creative as the artists' projects.

Even the priests of the art religion have lost their faith and are looking for other reasons to convince the masses. The Louvre, an institution whose very existence demands a belief in absolute hierarchy of worth, has trouble with the notion. It held a series of conferences and then released a volume titled "What Is a Masterpiece?" In that volume, Jean Galard put it like this:

> It is commonplace and convenient to say a film, a building or a book is a masterpiece: in other words that one places it among the works whose vast superiority, through excellence over all comers, one feels ready to proclaim. However, if forced to give one's arguments, if one has to make explicit the system (or at least the somewhat organized body of ideas) in which this excellence can be established, the idea of a master-piece becomes embarrassing. One might even say that, for many reasons, it seems completely indefensible.
>
> Firstly, by definition as we just saw, this idea supposes that one can make use of a principle of classification and ranking of works. However, any such principle would be of doubtful objectivity. A knowledge of history contradicts with all its force any hope for an objectivist aesthetic.[7]

In the rest of that volume, eminent art historians and curators try to explain how they can single out works in practice, even though there are no criteria to allow it in absolute theoretical terms. Particularly amusing is the article by Neil MacGregor,[8] which holds as a sign of the value of the altarpiece known as *The Wilton Diptych* the vast number of visitors who came to see it and the fact that it even appeared in a humorous cartoon in *The Spectator*. He writes, "only a masterpiece can touch each person in a unique way." Does this mean that iconic value is what makes a masterpiece? Does he really believe that (if the *Diptych* is a masterpiece now) it was not a masterpiece until the publicity department of the National Gallery managed to draw in 200,000 visitors? How good would the work have been if only 100,000 had come to see it and a few schoolchildren sketched it for art class? I do not mean to suggest that finding ways to engage the public with great art is not critically important, but you can't have it both ways. If it is only though appreciation by masses and by engagement with a social context that the art is great, then why go to the trouble? After all, the public will find a way to engage with something without any outside help, and we can then simply pronounce whatever that is "great."

This is essentially the advice Alice Marquis gives in her book. I don't think she really believes in the equality of everything either, however. She says again and again that the cultural "experts" make the wrong choices, that poor work is advanced. She bemoans the segregation of art into high and low, but what about good and bad (or great and mediocre)? What do any of these terms really mean? She says that at the extremes there might be some clarity: the difference between mud wrestling in a local bar and *King Lear* by the Royal Shakespeare Company, for example. But if we are to believe Jean Galard, then we will have trouble formulating a problem-free way of justifying our judgment even in these extreme cases. Yet it remains very difficult to get over the notion that there is in fact a difference and that it is not an entirely arbitrary construction. It is a grave error to consistently assume that the problems the arts have in relating to society today are mostly the result of infelicitous funding mechanisms or poor selection criteria; funding mechanisms have always been flawed and people have always made bad choices as well as good ones. The change is something more profound than all that.

I fear that for the music we are discussing to survive, it will be essential to convince even those who don't love it that this kind of difficult, nonfunctional, nonpopular art makes the world richer. Persuading someone to value and ultimately help support something they do not really care for will be no easy task, and it will take me most of this book to even attempt to do so. We must convince people that it has real value — not just to me or a handful of others like me, but in absolute terms. So let's see just how bad the situation is.

Our discussion cannot focus on purely aesthetic and artistic issues — it must address financial ones as well. Very few people object on principle to the existence of the kind of art that requires subsidies; what they object to is being asked to pay for it when they don't consume it. Marquis claims that the "arts have survived far longer without government intervention than with subsidies." But this is, of course, completely false as it relates to the kind of art I practice. The form of subsidy changes, but the arts as I mean them here (symphony orchestras, ballet companies, etc.) have always cost far more than they bring in, and society (whether in the form of a prince, a pope, a Rockefeller, a spouse who picks up the slack, or a Ministry of Culture) foots the bill. Moreover, in a time where wealth is less concentrated than in the past (at least in the more distant past), this inevitably means soliciting the patronage of people whose preferences are elsewhere.

You may notice that I am avoiding, and will go on avoiding, the question of exactly what sorts of public or private patronage would be ideal. I am not a public policy expert, and I believe that any scheme we create will have its advantages and disadvantages. My goal in this volume is to convince you that as a society it is worth it to continue trying to support this sort of noneconomically viable art. The broad acceptance of the general premise is what the art needs to survive, because it allows and even obliges those with the expertise and experience to keep looking for better models of sustaining subsidized art.

Lest we be tempted to spout something about diversity and say we should help preserve as many different kinds of music as possible — we should give all forms of expression a chance, and so on — we need to understand just how expensive Western classical art music is and how unlikely it is to survive without the patronage of society as a whole. We should begin this review with a conclusion, that reached by William Baumol and William Bowen in their report commissioned by the Twentieth Century Fund: *Performing Arts: The Economic Dilemma* (1966). They found that the performing arts will never be self-sufficient, because they are inherently labor intensive and cannot take advantage of economies of scale. As Alice Marquis pithily summarizes, "a string quartet must always have four players." Marquis and others, though, question this conclusion by suggesting that larger concert halls, recordings, television broadcasts, and so on, do in fact permit economies of scale. I suspect they would be right if we were dealing with a commodity. But as anyone who has sat in the Family Circle at the Metropolitan Opera knows, the experience is not the same as seeing an opera from the middle of the orchestra seats (although you don't have to take out a second mortgage to buy your tickets). It's not called "chamber music" for nothing, and intimacy is not only a preferable environment for some works, it is an integral component. In fact, by trying to seek supposed economies of scale, the largest arts organizations have made it so expensive to operate that they now have the perfect excuse not to let any untested new art through the door; it would be too big a risk to their entirely artificial bottom line.

Even in the most successful and populist-oriented arts groups, tickets are sold at a horrendous loss. Nonprofit theater ticket receipts represent on average 52 percent of the cost of opening the door; opera tickets — as expensive as they are — represent no more than 40 percent of the cost and often much less; symphony orchestra tickets represent less than 30 percent of the cost; and dance company tickets are a mere 27 percent of the cost.[9] But those are only best-case numbers for large, well-publicized organizations with conservative, market-considered programming, and they are from some time ago (the 1970s); the real situation is much worse. When I work with contemporary music ensembles, we do not even include in the budget any income from tickets. In the end we may realize a few hundred to a few thousand dollars on tickets if the concert is a great success. But $1,500 on tickets from a concert that costs $45,000 to produce is too insignificant to even calculate a percentage. Moreover, I think that is exactly the point.

We can't support this art in the long run based on the math that Marquis cites so thoroughly, because there is no market-based reason to do any of this:

> In a survey in 1993, the National Cultural Alliance, using highly leading questions that should have favored the arts, found that only 5 percent of the population was "extremely interested" in the arts and humanities and that even among the more affluent and educated only 30 percent would even claim to be "very interested." 57 percent say that the arts and humanities play at most a minor role in their lives.[10]

Marquis is not painting an unrealistically bleak picture when she recounts the story of when the first President Bush, after holding a luncheon for the ten very eminent winners of that year's National Arts Medal, stood up and said "All right you artists, now I want you to meet some real artists!" With that, Joe DiMaggio and Ted Williams entered the room to accompany President Bush to a baseball game. The arts are simply not a significant part of most people's lives, even among our leaders.

In 1974, Joseph Rody found that, after more then ten years of out-reach by the NEA, only 1 percent of the population had attended a single symphony orchestra concert.[11] So, why do we keep going back to marketing analyses or arguments? So what if you manage to entice 1.2 percent of the population instead of 1.1 percent to attend an arts pro-gram? So what if you lose only $30 per ticket sold instead of $32? There has to be another reason why we're doing this.

It seems clear that even with fantastically effective arts education and outreach, this kind of art has never and probably will never interest the majority and perhaps not even a significant minority of the population (at least not one willing to do more than attend the occasional block-buster museum exhibit once every couple of years). Moreover, even if we could interest these masses, the kind of arts developed in the West over the last few hundred years probably still would not be self-supporting.

Another market argument is often made in favor of the arts, and I'd like to eliminate that as well. That argument is not so much in favor of the arts as it is in favor of the buildings that house the arts. Boosters claim enormous financial gains to regions that construct arts facilities (both direct gains in tourism and taxes and indirect gains in property values and quality of life). The multibillion-dollar redevelopment of New York's Upper West Side after the construction of Lincoln Center is a classic example. While this argument may be more viable politi-cally than "art for art's sake," one has to wonder about how economi-cally valid it really is. What is often left out of these arguments are the enormous tax subsidies that go to the arts (yes, even here in America) in the form of tax breaks on contributions to nonprofit organizations, land concessions, discount postal rates, and so on. Any equivalent redi-rection of tax dollars to an area might well produce similar effects. More important, if this is really the argument, and no more reason exists to support the arts than to support more playgrounds or a sports stadium, or perhaps even a shopping mall, then the battle has already been lost. When the only medical argument that can made for a cough syrup is that it also contains alcohol, one has to wonder whether there might not be other ways to get drunk.

As a society, the only reason to go to all this trouble and spend all this money is that the result has great worth — not economic worth, but cultural value. However we can no longer really evaluate cultural value, and therefore it cannot easily figure into our calculations as a society. (For an individual, especially one who does not care for this supposedly "valuable" art, this concept is even harder to accept. I'll try to offer some arguments in the coming chapters as to why I think you might and how your personal taste and my rather abstract notions of aesthetic value can interact.)

This reticence should not be surprising; it results almost inevitably from a situation where the public is no longer willing simply to take someone else's word on whether they should see or hear something. Today we want to decide for ourselves; we're a democracy, after all. "Choice" is the word of the day, and how can one object to it without seeming to be some sort of arch-reactionary snob who wants to force his taste on others? But there's the rub; the whole market-driven system happens to also be predicated on a basic belief that is entirely incompatible with the idea of intrinsic value or worth. Under a market system, one must absolutely believe that there is no worth other than what someone will pay for something (its market value). A seat at the symphony is worth $40 if that's what the ticket can be sold for. If it costs $75 per seat to put on the concert, that just shows how badly run the groups are, or how much better they need to become at marketing or branding, or that they simply ought not to exist: They are not "viable." Value outside a market has no meaning.

If I want to maintain that the arts require the existence of another sort of value that is intrinsic to the works — and if I am not advocating a full-scale return to a hierarchical worldview where it is closeness to God or the word of a prince that conveys this value — where does this value come from? How can we justify the value of one work over another without succumbing to the pitfalls of objectivist aesthetics that (as Jean Galard reminds us) are bound to fail in time?

I would like to address this problem in two different ways, and both of them require the same first step: We must correct Kuhn's error. We must abandon an absolutist view of relativism. It seems to me that we can perfectly well judge one theory to be truer than another without claiming that we have found the final Truth, or that such a thing is even possible. If a current theory in physics corresponds to the results of experiments out to thirteen decimal places, I am willing to say it's "true." Moreover, if physicists work out the details of string theory and find that it subsumes the former theory's results while using fewer experimentally determined variables (more of it comes from the structure of the theory directly) and now allows us to make accurate predictions to fifteen decimal places, I will be happy to say it is more "true." That the two theories imply slightly incompatible physical systems, and that even the new theory will undoubtedly be further revised, does not (at least for me) undermine my willingness to believe in the greater truth of the more refined theory. We are all willing to get on airplanes made with theories that we know in advance are not true, but merely true enough to work for that application (most aerodynamic problems are solved with approximate answers that can be calculated on ever smaller grids of points — say, along the surface of the wing). I certainly would not want to be the test pilot on the helicopter that da Vinci made using the theories of aerodynamics of his time — advanced though he was in relation to his contemporaries.

The same notion of "more" and "less" true might have a parallel in the arts. Rather than seeking a perfect set of guidelines, we could choose to accept theories or aesthetic frameworks that allow us to make judgments with some amount of validity — even if these frameworks themselves cannot be absolutely and timelessly true. Were we to make this leap, the kinds of useful approximations of truth we are familiar with in science might also become available as tools for evaluating the worth of art, or what Habermas in a perversely poetic way referred to as the "amount of Beauty." We must accept that these systems are not now and can never be perfect, however. Perhaps physics will have a final, perfect "Theory of Everything," but the arts will not. Our individual ideas of beauty and meaning are too twisted and blown by our culture and our personal history — not to mention the bias that taste inflicts on even our most objective judgments — to hope for a final "Theory of Aesthetic Value." Nonetheless, we can have and *have* had skewed, incomplete, biased — albeit useful and meaningful — theories. Furthermore, our inability to determine with precision the intrinsic value of a work does not mean that its worth is nil or entirely relative, or that it is impossible to make meaningful approximations of its worth relative to other works.

Even if you're willing to go along with me up to this point we still have a real problem: What are these theories supposed to be measuring, albeit imperfectly? In the case of science, we can suppose that the theories are approximating a physical reality. I suspect that even the most dedicated and dogmatic postmodernist does not really stop to gather his or her socially constructed thoughts before turning on the light switch — for fear that otherwise electricity might suddenly cease to exist. I find it extremely compelling to believe that, in fact, a world exists out there, and that this world appears to be largely constant, regardless of our mental states and cultural constructs. That is not to say that mental states and cultural constructs are not real and powerful, but that — while those constructs and states affect how we perceive and interpret the world — the physical world (call it Truth in this context) is largely indifferent to those beliefs.[12]

All right, you say, even if I buy this, what about beauty or, to use a less loaded term, aesthetic value? As I have mentioned, I have two possible answers. These are not theories about measuring aesthetic value, but theories about why one might believe that intrinsic, aesthetic value could exist at all, independently from sociocultural values. I am hoping to avoid the error of trying to badger you into agreeing with me about a set of specific aesthetic judgments, because such agreements are short-lived. Ultimately, Harold Bloom is probably right when he writes that: "Pragmatically, aesthetic value can be recognized or experienced, but it cannot be conveyed [...] To quarrel on its behalf is always a blunder."[13] But we cannot escape the question, What could aesthetic value possibly be and why ever would one believe that it exists?

One theory I can offer as to why beauty and aesthetic value exist abstractly is that they are part of the human mind. In other words, they are the inevitable result of the operation of natural aspects of human cognitive universals within aesthetic domains. Linguist Noam Chomsky famously claimed that aliens coming to Earth would judge us to all be speaking dialects of a single human universal language. He believed that the structure of this Universal Grammar was the result of our human perceptual apparatus coupled with our mental language organ (a simple example of the universality of human languages is the consistent division of reality into nouns [things] and verbs [actions] rather than into some sort of imaginable composites that mix those two notions, although the similarities go much deeper). He claims that all of the apparent diversity on the surface of languages is the result of a more unified set of tools and rules at lower cognitive levels.

I suspect, though I certainly cannot prove, that a similar universal aesthetic organ (or perhaps several suborgans) exists in the human mind. While different "dialects" may implement very different forms of aesthetic systems, as do the different manifestations of human language, they all share some of the same structural underpinnings. Although this does not necessarily imply that we are all artists, it should at least mean that we are all capable of being art appreciators. We must remember, though, that just as not everyone is drawn to literature, or even puns for that matter, the range of uses each individual applies to the art faculty are as shaped by personality, culture, and experience as our applications of language faculties.[14]

A basic feeling for the universality of aesthetics can be achieved by comparing a visit to a natural history museum with a visit to any museum of ancient arts or culture. At the natural history museum, some objects may seem beautiful, others frightening. Many may appear strange while some are familiar. It is clear to me that I am imposing these sensations; I am giving those "meanings" to the pile of bones or colored rock in front of me. To really make sense of what we are seeing, we need quite a lot of information (fortunately supplied on the placards next to the exhibits). At the museum of ancient art, the sensation is entirely different. Look at objects from any culture, recent or ancient, and I defy you to feel them as wholly strange or foreign. One always experiences at least some sense of familiarity with even the most exotic objects. And why shouldn't there be, because we know that hands and minds very much like our own formed these objects? Whether symmetrical or wildly irregular, we see a form created by a human mind. Whether it is simple and elegant or ornamental and rich, we can recognize aesthetic intentions. Certainly, we cannot instantly judge what is the best of each kind of work (although we may have gut preferences), but it is clear that there are differing degrees of achievement. More important, it is easy to imagine that with more time and more context (knowledge) our appreciation could deepen. This is not so with the fossils down the street. No matter how much we learn about dinosaurs, or how much we might appreciate the rarity or scientific importance of a particular exhibit, it feels artificial to speak of its beauty. Beauty in this aesthetic sense is not just in the eye of the beholder, but also in the eye of the maker; it is the product of the human creative spirit.

To be perfectly clear, I believe that if there were extraterrestrial intelligent beings and if they were to judge our arts, they would most likely find them completely baffling and might never be able to understand the aesthetic criteria that let us say one imperfect representation of nature is better than another. Fortunately for us, though, we are not extraterrestrials; we happen to be human just like the maker of the artwork. The calipers with which these absolute intrinsic values can be measured, at least approximately, can perhaps be made with our own human minds. It seems perfectly plausible (although perhaps not proven) that our sense of beauty and our need to create could be as much a product of our native gifts as the ability to learn language or walk upright on two feet.

Now, any specific theory about how this sense works and what specifically it says about one work of art or another may still be very problematic. This is why I have no intention of offering even my best theories of what artistic criteria we should use to judge art. Any of the deficiencies you might find with my proposed guidelines could be used to undermine the broader argument about the ability to approximate meaningfully (even though problematically) such judgments. These approximate theories do, however, at least potentially provide a framework in which one work could be better, more perfect, or more beautiful than another, in a sense that goes beyond a specific cultural framework.

I know that most people are not content with this answer. The idea of cognitive universals can be hard for many people to accept, especially when used to account for any but the most trivial aspects of human activity. Perhaps an even greater problem is that other types of cognitive abilities do not yield hierarchical judgments like "better" and "worse." Even though we may speak of more and less correct use of language, most linguists would argue that as long as enough people agree, the mistake can, in time, become the rule. I don't think either of these problems is ultimately fatal, however. I believe that cognitive universals have far-ranging repercussions for human activity and that it is possible for the human mind to contain biases toward configurations of sounds or objects that might lead to some things being more beautiful or fascinating than others, even than others that we prefer (because they are more useful, or familiar, or comforting, or remind us of something specific). But, if you just don't buy any of this, I have one last proposition to offer you. I offer a choice, just like Morpheus did in the *Matrix*: You can take the red pill or the blue pill, but either way you're going to have to live on in the world you chose. This is the artistic or aesthetic version of Pascal's wager, only this time neither choice is without risk.

In many ways any big choice about how we organize our society will boil down to choosing the kind of world we want to live in and the premises it needs to exist. Hobbes's "social contract" sees us as trading in our "natural state" of freedom for peace, so perhaps we need to construct a parallel "aesthetic contract" that would acknowledge the tradeoffs we must make if we want to fill our nasty, brutish, and short lives with wonderful art. This is what I meant when I implied that it doesn't really matter whether the NEA is purveying fictions, as long as they are fictions that make the world better. There is a fairly recent novel called *The Life of Pi*, which tells of a similar choice involving how a grown man should remember a trauma he suffered as a boy, and relating this choice to believing in God. Ultimately, the author suggests, the only way to avoid falling into despair is to believe in a world where there is reason for hope, justified or not.

In other domains, such as morality, the acceptance of an unprovable set of intrinsic values represents the norm and is clearly advantageous to society. For example, most of us believe that the gratuitous murder of another human being is not simply wrong because a deity or a law says so; we believe that in some way it is intrinsically wrong. Whether or not this view is true (we wouldn't think of a lion killing another lion to establish its territory as wrong), the world is a much safer and I believe better place while we hold this belief. Moreover, as a society we have such a strong belief in the rightness (or at least utility) of this view that we are willing to lock away in jail or kill those individuals who disagree.

It is a useful exercise to perform a thought experiment. We should imagine that there are, in fact, intrinsic values, or at least that we are all willing to act as if there are (the distinction between these two worlds would probably be impossible to detect). Don't worry for the moment where these values come from or how to evaluate them. Let's just contrast, in our imaginations, a world that acts as if it believes in intrinsic aesthetic values with one that does not.

What happens if intrinsic values truly exist, or if we at least believe that they do? This view has led schools to force children to read Shakespeare and college students to read James Joyce. The idea is that whether they enjoy them or not, these works are somehow important.

Even in the United States (one of the few countries that does not see the need for a cabinet-level guardian of culture), presidents have invited orchestras to play whether or not they liked orchestral music; John F. Kennedy had an aide who told him when to clap so as not to embarrass himself. Families have dragged children to operas, museums, and ballets.

Furthermore, the idea of intrinsic value has by no means been limited to "high culture"; it has had an equally profound effect on even the most commercial of art forms. Guys have tried to impress their dates by taking them to jazz clubs instead of going to hear a Bee Gees cover band. Rock fans who aimed at sophistication have sought out more ambitious "underground" music and were quick to display their highly developed taste to their friends. Liking the most popular or accessible group was often seen as a sign of superficiality. Generally, people felt that if they got nothing out of more "difficult" art, the problem was likely their own. After enough time, some, perhaps even many, might make it over the hurdles and come to love "it" — whether "it" is John Donne, Richard Wagner, or John Coltrane, and regardless of whether they want to tell a survey taker that arts and humanities play a major role in their life.

On the other hand, what happens if there are no intrinsic values or if we act as if there were none? Then it seems a waste of time to grapple with much of anything. People will need to have a wide menu of choices. If something doesn't satisfy them, they'll flick to another channel, and if nothing good can be found on any channel, the search itself becomes the program. The father of President George W. Bush was known to prefer the Beach Boys to the Philharmonic and saw no need to pretend a love for high culture: If he didn't like broccoli, he just wouldn't eat it. To him the true artists are baseball players, because he likes baseball.

The lesson that has been taken from John Cage and Marcel Duchamp's attacks on the artistic status quo (placing a urinal in a museum display, or claiming that traffic noise was as much music as Mozart) is that if a urinal or traffic noise could be appreciated aesthetically in any way, then they must therefore be the equal of Mozart and Rembrandt as must be Garth Brooks and black velvet Elvises. This view quickly leads to taste being the only legitimate arbiter. With current distribution schemes, this leads to the downward homogenizing of taste toward the lowest common denominator, a phenomenon that makes almost everyone vaguely uncomfortable.

But even in a techno-utopian future where content on demand lets each person's taste be perfectly satisfied — those who like Schoenberg and those who prefer Billy Ray Cyrus — there may not be any place left for art. Art is not about giving people what they want. It's about giving them something *they don't know they want*. It's about submitting to someone else's vision; forcing your aesthetic sense to assimilate the output of someone else's. And if there is not even the possibility of a really valuable return, why bother? Certainly, why pay for it?

The lesson I take from Cage and Duchamp is not that all art is equal, but that all art demands a surrendering of your vision in submission to the artist's or at least the museum or concert curator's. Duchamp dares you to see the beauty he found in a urinal or a shovel, or perhaps he wants you to see the absurdity he sees in the whole museum setting as a way of perceiving. Cage tries to force you to turn the same ears to the traffic that you would give to Mozart. They both know that art is a team effort between artist and audience and that the latter sometimes needs help in understanding the importance and nature of its role. This is not to say that Cage and Duchamp are necessarily great artists, but they understood how difficult it is to engage with art. They lived in the world where art could be great — even as they were trying to subvert one particular theory of what might constitute art.

Some of us, even today, may have waded through *Finnegan's Wake* or *A la recherche du temps perdu*, but how many would read such difficult works, demanding that level of investment, knowing that ultimately they could not, even potentially, offer anything more than a John Grisham novel (which, after all, already offers all the benefits of a Grisham novel without all that extra difficulty)? Even just the knowledge that in all likelihood they were complex dross (as inevitably will often be the case with new art) would make it all but impossible.

Most artworks are mediocre, if not downright bad! This idea, which is shocking to many people, will be true whether or not there are abstract criteria by which to judge how absolutely awful they are. We think of art as the great masterworks we know, but it's very easy to forget the mountains of mediocrity that were sifted to lift Bach or Dante or Emily Dickinson to their Olympian heights. I have heard people suggest that the gene pool has somehow been diluted, through massive population growth in the twentieth century, to the point that no more Beethovens are possible (this came from a composer). What they forget is that even if you had been living in Beethoven's time, it is not certain that is what you would have heard when you went to a concert. Gioacchino Rossini was arguably more famous than Beethoven in the early nineteenth century and the French opera composer Giacomo Meyerbeer was much more popular than his German rival Richard Wagner, and that is before we even start naming the legions of widely performed mediocrities whose works have mercifully been consigned to history's dustbin.

It is easy to forget how, at any given time, the sheer mass of bad or mediocre work tends to dwarf the good or great works. This can lead us to assume that the past was somehow better, because we remember only the best parts. I would venture to say, however, that there have certainly been more masterpieces created during the past twenty years than were made during the last twenty years of the nineteenth century (an easy bet because the population is so much bigger now). We just haven't finished sifting out the gems from the garbage yet, and if we believe that gems are not really there to be found, we might as well not bother.

Imagine having to go through the 50 million paintings — probably a very low estimate — done last year by everyone from famous artists to unknown talents to my ninety-something-year-old grandmother (who paints as a retirement hobby). Even if you knew there were a *Guernica* hiding in there somewhere, which of course you wouldn't, how would you keep your eyes fresh enough to see it? And if you don't think art is anything more than a cabal designed to extort subsidies from the public, why even try?

However, if no one were willing make this enormous effort or to carry forward with a belief that there really is something special to some works, even before 200,000 people had seen them and humorous cartoons of them have appeared in *The Spectator*, most great new works would never be discovered. Difficult works, like those of Joyce or Proust (or Schoenberg or Messiaen), would become completely impossible to find, and perhaps also to produce.

This is why culture became an undemocratic realm in the first place, and why any attempts to democratize it may bear unwanted side effects. To find great art, we need people who are able and willing to go through those 50 million paintings on the off-chance of finding one masterpiece. This screening process means that when you or I decide to spend time on art, we can reduce our choices to works that have already been evaluated and recommended. Someone — presumably someone who has demonstrated a greater knowledge of this realm than we possess — thinks they are worth spending time on. They can't know if we will like them, but they have judged that these works possess value.

I'm not saying that the system was ever perfect. Individuals will always try to advance their friends and punish their enemies. But the pressure not to be left out of an important (read: valuable) trend, and the desire to find the next big thing, will force some degree of integrity and openness in even the most corrupt arts administrators. Ultimately, it is in their interest to promote as "great" things that truly are. But when the so-called authorities buy into the idea that nothing is intrinsically worth more than anything else, they become a negative force. They're no longer trying to find great works and expose them to the public; they're just hoping to impose their tastes, promote their political or social agendas, or simply get rich and famous. This is how Dr. Marquis sees the NEA: a bumbling, unethical, unhelpful force.

The lack of a belief in intrinsic value does not only affect so-called high arts. The same deleterious effects are appearing in more popular art forms like jazz or film or some kinds of pop music. Perhaps because these forms don't make quite the same outrageous demands on listeners, viewers, or the society that subsidizes them — and I mean that in the best possible sense — the process doesn't seem to be as far along. Still, around the world Hollywood blockbuster productions increasingly dominate the market, driving the various traditions of art cinema to the margins. Jazz, which requires an enormous amount of knowledge and connoisseurship to appreciate in-depth, seems to be fighting for its survival — in constant danger of becoming upscale aural wallpaper or getting moved into the same prison/museums that have locked innovation out of the symphony orchestra. There seem to be fewer and fewer hardcore buffs who scour the clubs, sure that another Coltrane or Miles Davis is waiting to be found.

In jazz and rock, the work itself and the performance of the work are joined in a way that is quite different from the case in theater or classical music. That relationship may blur some of the distinctions I have been making and certainly complicates the sort of atemporal judgments I've been describing; however, I don't believe it fundamentally alters them. When high school students start broadening their record collections and searching for more adventurous artists they haven't heard before, they do so because they believe that great things are to be found out there, things with real value. Once that belief disappears, turning on top-40 radio will be enough.

Real art cannot be an act of manipulation or marketing, but only an act of faith — faith that great art is something truly remarkable; faith that someone, somewhere, sometime might make the effort to understand what an artist has to offer and not merely seek what is already known and liked.

It requires a tremendous leap of faith to surrender control of our perception to someone else, on the off-chance that he may offer us something we never knew we wanted but now would not want to be without. We are risking our time, our attention, our money, and our frustration. If we don't believe at all anymore in the inherent value and transformative potential of art, then why would anyone in his right mind take the risk?

If we could turn back the history of the human race and run it over again, I'm very doubtful that anything like the Western artistic tradition would happen twice. You might think that aesthetic values as I have described, if real, should inevitably lead to some similar outcome, whatever the cost, but the structural principles that allow skyscrapers hardly guarantee a society willing to pour money into building 100-story towers. A cultural form that serves no obvious function, does not appeal to most of the population, and is so expensive that it can never support itself seems like such an aberration. Yet, those of us who believe there truly are aesthetic values can see that this odd form of expression, which sets a tiny handful of individual humans free to pursue their own visions of aesthetic achievement without regard to taste, understanding, and practicality, has given us an astounding body of work. Ovid said: "Nothing is of more use to man than the arts which have no utility." In an age when we spend so much on so many things, it would be a terrible shame to give up completely on something that can bring society moments and objects of such value.

2

TASTE

… you encounter a stranger, an uncanny startlement rather than a fulfill-
ment of expectations.

— **Harold Bloom**

Let's assume, at least for argument's sake, that you're willing to consider that something like aesthetic value might exist, or that it would be
beneficial to pretend that it exists. Either way, we still need to explore
why more people aren't clambering to acquire as much of this supposed
value as possible: If it is so valuable in the abstract, why is it not more
personally attractive to many people? In other words, we need (at least
partially) to account for the thing that there's no accounting for: taste.

To deal with taste, we need to differentiate several entangled concepts. These concepts have been the subjects of entire books, and I have
no intention of giving them anything approaching such comprehen-
sive treatment here. I am simply trying to specify my meanings for the
purposes of the present discussion, to avoid confusion and misunder-
standing. First are the notions of art and culture. I will avoid the term
"culture" as much as possible, because the broad (societal) meaning and

the narrow (art-related) meanings are too intertwined in our "cultural" (academic meaning) discourse.

Although it presents many of the same difficulties, the word "art" will be impossible to avoid. For present purposes I'd like to define "art" in a very limited way as an aesthetic object (i.e., an object produced with an aesthetic intent) either produced by humans or by following instructions produced by humans (e.g., a computer program used to create an image). I will also use the word in the context of collections of such objects or the quest to produce such objects. I realize that many other definitions are possible and perhaps preferable in a general context — especially since the early part of the twentieth century when the centrality of objects over processes came into question. As I will touch upon the latter point in the next chapter, however, for now please bear with this very limited use of the word "art." If I don't limit our meaning from the start, we are all too likely to fall into playing a game of "art is _____," which never seems to yield much insight.

The next term needed for our discussion, "entertainment," can cause real confusion. Although art may be entertaining, by my definition art is not entertainment. I define, in this context, entertainment as either the subjective feeling one experiences while doing something enjoyable (potentially, though certainly not necessarily, while engaging with art) or as objects and activities designed to produce enjoyment in the user, consumer, or observer. Because I have defined aesthetic intent as central to art and diversionary intent as central to entertainment, they could be considered separate categories, if we were able to determine intent perfectly and if it weren't so easy to have multiple, simultaneous intentions for the same act or object. I am the first to admit that much entertainment has a high degree of (presumably intentional) aesthetic value and that much art has (also presumably intentional) diversionary utility. Nonetheless, in many if not most cases, the primary intent, artistic or entertainment-related, is discernable and we can consider these as two separable categories.

Confusion between art and entertainment pervades much of the discourse on "high" versus "low" art or culture. According to my definitions, no high or low art exists per se, but certainly good and bad art (or at least better and worse) does; difficult and accessible art perhaps also does. Whether the medium is graffiti or carved Carrara marble, aesthetic intent creates art. Herbert Gans's book *Popular Culture and High Culture*[1] is a good example of the high/low culture discourse genre. Gans mixes metaphors of programming and consumption with ideas like art and aesthetics in a way that clarifies neither and obscures both. Gans sets out with what I suppose he views as the noble intent of defending popular culture from the attacks and condescension of "High Culture." But his fears strike me as comical (perhaps in 1974 when the first edition was published this would have been less the case). One hardly needs to defend the choices of the overwhelming majority over those of a curmudgeonly few. Popularity, in this context, is its own unassailable defense. If enough individuals, commanding enough resources, enjoy it enough to support it, it will exist in a free market society. The threat is elsewhere.

Whether we call art and culture high or low, those things that cannot support themselves in the marketplace are threatened. We must decide whether in some cases artistic or aesthetic value ought to override economic value and popular preference in the allocation of society's resources. In other words, we need to ask, "Why should I pay (or help to pay) for something that I don't like?" The first step toward answering this question is to address the underlying paradox: If it's really better in a meaningful way, why don't I prefer it? Unless I can satisfactorily answer this first question, it will be very hard to continue onward to the benefits, other than sheer satisfaction or diversion, that might justify continued support.

To approach an answer, we must admit to human fallibility. Judgments made by you or me or the curatorial staff at New York's Museum of Modern Art, in good faith, can be wrong. Even if intrinsic, absolute aesthetic values do exist, our individual or collective judgments about a given work will often be incorrect. What we took for the "emperor's new clothes" might turn out to be a shadow on that poor, old, deceived emperor who now appears naked after all. However, if we assume that all artistic assessments are probably wrong — a sort of artistic *caveat emptor* — we may foreclose many possibilities in advance. As Harold Bloom wrote, "great art is strange" (he was actually writing about canonical literature, but I will extend his lovely sentiment). This doesn't mean that art has to be innovative or different in that sense, but it is always at least deeply personal and of itself, and thus a little off from anything we might expect. It places our aesthetic senses in a configuration they have never experienced before, except perhaps with the same work at an earlier time. This is not always very comfortable or entertaining. In fact, if one is not in the right mood it might be downright irritating.

This strangeness that comes with great art is a big part of the reason we often hesitate to approach such works.

As Henry James wrote in the preface to *The Wings of the Dove*:

> The enjoyment of a work of art, the acceptance of an irresistible illusion, constituting, to my sense, our highest experience of "luxury," the luxury is not greatest by my consequent measure, when the work asks for as little attention as possible. It is greatest, it is delightfully divinely great, when we feel the surface, like the thick ice of the skater's pond, bear without cracking the strongest pressure we throw on it. The sound of the crack one may recognize, but never surely to call it a luxury.[2]

The sound of the crack is of course our normal expectation. It is what ought to happen, if we had not moved into that very strange (to James, luxurious) place where art lives. The price we must pay for that luxury is the effort of our attention and concentration. We must throw our strongest pressure against the ice to see if it is, in fact, capable of resisting.

Modern life puts us in a sort of double bind. An enormously stressful, constantly changing work and personal life is coupled with an unprecedented amount of "leisure" time. This often leaves little or no mental energy for consumption in each "free" hour. Therefore, we (myself included) quite reasonably seek to fill much of our leisure time with light entertainments: things that will occupy and divert us. Although these entertainments may well have some aesthetic value, that is not why we choose them and it is not the way we are using them. Art, in the way I refer to it is, as the Marxist critics decry, a bourgeois activity in that it requires real leisure, both mental and physical, to make and to appreciate. Only those able to give their full attention and concentration, without a reward of any concrete utility, can really experience art. A deep aesthetic experience of even the most accessible art is exhausting and consuming. Glancing at the paintings in an art exhibition or playing Mozart as background music is perhaps entertainment, but the experience is not the experience of art.

You may at this point quite reasonably say, "But I have, at least occasionally, made such an effort and I still didn't like it." How much is enough effort before I call the supposed experts' bluff? Although I don't have one clear solution for this dilemma, I do have a guiding principle that bears upon it: "The Chinese Food Effect."

I distinctly recall a big banquet dinner at a local Chinese restaurant when I was a child. In addition to my parents and siblings, my maternal grandparents were there. My grandparents (especially my grandfather), like many of their generation, were extremely leery of "ethnic food." I remember peppering my grandparents with questions both during and after the meal to determine whether they liked the food or whether our efforts to force them to try this or that dish had yielded only the polite endurance of an unpleasant taste. I felt for the longest time that they were avoiding the questions, giving me evasive responses. Perhaps they were too polite to come out and say how awful everything tasted to them. As I persisted, however (and I was nothing if not a persistent child), a different sort of understanding dawned on me: They didn't actually know if they liked it or not.

When my grandparents tasted this deeply unfamiliar food, the sensation of difference or unfamiliarity overwhelmed all other sensations. I assume that this is what people mean when they say that all classical music (or all country music, for that matter) sounds the same to them. They are saying that the difference from their norm is so great that difference is their only salient perception.

They may also be saying something more subtle. They probably do not yet have the categories they would need to parse the experience into meaningful units. Cognitive science suggests that we can't really think about too many things at once, no matter the context.[3] Instead, we employ various sorts of mental data reduction techniques, such as categorical perception and something psychologists call "chunking." Even chess grandmasters do not really hold in their head the next 350 moves; they have chunked together families of possible moves into a still large, but less superhuman number of categories. This is not a conscious strategy we decide to employ; it is an inevitable part of the way we process our enormously complex environment. It does require experience, however, or at least repeated exposure.

After eating a dozen Chinese meals, perhaps in a few different restaurants, one can start to form some reasonable expectations about the next meal. Some of these may well prove false, but expectations will form nonetheless and gradually more reliable ones will take the place of those that are debunked. You may notice that the starch served is always rice, until one day you are served noodles; however, you can still probably hold on to the idea that they will not give you potatoes. You may start grouping the kinds of dishes you eat into categories, perhaps by the type of sauce: sweet-and-sour dishes, soy sauce-based dishes, steamed dishes with dipping sauce. Moreover, within each category you can now make and remember many finer judgments: the sweet-and-sour sauces here are a little on the gloppy side; this dish is very spicy whereas it is a dish that is usually mild; this dish has a strongly scented spice in it (maybe star anise). I've probably already pushed the analogy too far, but once you get some bearing, I suspect that in a cuisine that covers most of a continent and was developed by one the most ancient civilizations on Earth, there are things for everyone to love (my grandfather became especially partial to sweet-and-sour fish).

This principle in application puts a real burden on those who program and present art. They have to astutely mix repetition with discovery, all the while knowing that no one can attend every concert. Neither an ever-changing smorgasbord nor a constant diet of comfort food (the two most commonly offered options) will really help someone develop his or her palate.

But what does it mean for you as a receiver of art? How many meals that lead to a night of indigestion must you endure before you can legitimately call it quits and say, this is just not for me? No single answer works for everyone, but I have a rule of thumb: Keep trying until you've gotten past the threshold I'm calling "The Chinese Food Effect." By the time you can clearly remember details about works in a given genre, when you can compare and contrast them to other more or less closely related works, you are at least seeing the aesthetic object not only through its deviation from your expectations. If by that point the genre or style of work is still unsatisfying, it may not be for you. As universal as I believe human aesthetics to be, we are all still very different individuals. Each of us has been shaped by particular endowments and experiences. Some of us may simply be lactose intolerant when it comes to a given type of expression. I suspect, though, that once you have explored a few kinds of cuisine you may start to see what one might love even in dishes that may be too spicy for you.

I believe that the investment of time it may take to explore something really new rewards one with enormous gains. Even more than reconsidering the works you love, exploring a whole new artistic terrain is a staggeringly powerful experience. I am tempted to cite the studies about greater stimulation increasing the production of new neurons in rat brains, but that's not really the point. The point is that wonderful luxury of Henry James, if you're ready to exert the strongest pressure.

If all you need to do is take a walk, a treadmill or a small park will do. But we need places like Yellowstone, Patagonia, or the Galapagos to show us the extraordinary range of nature's possibilities. So, too, our aesthetic sense can be adequately exercised most of the time with the stimulation of entertainment we enjoy and the discoveries of everyday existence. But every so often, when you've saved up your pennies and energies and want to go someplace extraordinary, you're willing to put up with the discomfort and inconvenience of traveling so you can go to someplace strange and new. That's the goal of subsidized art — to provide those really exotic locales that you may never see but that can make you dream by just being out there.

3

CONCEPT AND CRAFT

The artistic communication is cut: it no longer exists. The object presented no longer has any aesthetic, moral, marketable, or consumable function. It is solely and undisputedly there for nothing. The observer finds that he is alone with himself and confronted with himself in front of an anonymous thing that gives him no solution. Art is no longer there. It's about something else.

[...]

My position is the logical conclusion based on art history and its apparent contradictions. [...] Chance, inspiration, and the right moment must be forsaken for a theory, and art is not capable of this.[1]

— **Daniel Buren**

Until now I have tried not to bring specific styles, aesthetics, or techniques into the discussion. One trend within the arts has done so much to undermine the very premises of subsidized nonfunctional art, however, that I feel the need to address it. More damning than any other criticism of subsidized art is the idea that artists are simply charlatans out to bilk our patrons with aesthetic snake oil. In earlier times when craft was a more overt component of a piece of art, this critique did not really exist. The notion of an art that is purely conceptual, however, opened this floodgate.

The Conceptual art movement had its heyday from about the mid-1960s to the late 1970s, but the ideas that led to the movement were already apparent in the early part of the century. Surrealism, Marcel Duchamp, John Cage, Fluxus, and many other individuals and movements had already embraced large parts of what would become the full Conceptual credo. Even now, more than twenty years after the tide has turned against this attitude/approach, museum shows are still highly influenced by the Conceptual revolution brought about by these artists who in essence do not believe in art.

Let's look at an "important" piece of Conceptual art by Lawrence Weiner:

> One Hole in the Ground Approximately 1'x1'x1'. One Gallon Water Based White Paint Poured into this Hole.

This is neither just a mental exercise, nor is it a set of instructions. It is all and none of these things at once. Here is Weiner's declaration of intent relative to these works (there were many such pieces):

> 1. The artist may construct the piece.
> 2. The piece may be fabricated.
> 3. The piece need not be built.

> Each being equal and consistent with the intent of the artist, the decision as to the condition rests with the receiver upon the occasion of receivership.[2]

Weiner really seems intent on preserving all possible ambiguity. In an interview from 1972, he said, "I don't care aesthetically which of the three conditions the work exists in. It would be a fascistic gesture on my part if I were to say you can accept the things only on a verbal information level, which would be type on a page, or you can accept them only on an aural information level. It doesn't matter whether it is conveyed verbally or aurally." Later in the same interview, he amplified the meaning: "There's no way to build a piece incorrectly." For Weiner and for (most if not all of) the Conceptualists, the question is not art, it is art's use in and by society. They believe that the necessary role of the artist has become that of a social critic. They believe the creation of objects with aesthetic or expressive value is an anathema.

In that same interview Weiner said:

> Anyone who imposes a unique condition for receivership, for interpretation for seeing a work, is placing art within a context that is almost 19th century. There is the specific, unique, emotional object produced by a prophet, produced by the only person who can make this. It becomes Expressionist to say: "I am the only one who can make this work, there's no other viable means of doing it." I find Expressionism related to aesthetic fascism. And being basically a Marxist, I find any kind of Expressionism fascist. It becomes a moral issue as well as an aesthetic one.[3]

I have quoted at some length, because I feared that some readers unfamiliar with this sort of discourse would assume any summary I might make to be hyperbole. Unfortunately, though, it is almost impossible to exaggerate the rhetoric of these social critics–cum-artists beyond what they have done themselves.

In Chapter 2, I mentioned that, in a certain way, art is bourgeois: In other words, it is a luxury. Although art consumes some societal resources, it does not directly improve the lot of the suffering masses. Art will not feed the hungry, and, though it was tried during the French Revolution, it does not make a very efficient source of heat when burned. The artists of the Conceptual art movement decided that this was not a situation that could be accepted. The societal respect accrued by Romantic artists through the nineteenth century gave the artist a privileged position in modern society. Although these new Conceptual artists thought of Romantic art as representing everything they despised, they were more than happy to make use of this public visibility, or at least legitimacy. In fact, the public nature of the artist's role became the most important thing for the Conceptual artists. They would use their art to show the world that "art was no longer there. It's about something else," as Daniel Buren said in the quote that opens this chapter. I'm tempted to equate their posture with that of a petulant child overturning the board of a game they no longer want to play, so

that everyone else must also stop. I believe their critique does, however, contain at least a grain of something more serious, so it is worth
exploring a bit more why this happened and where their mistake lies.
I believe that there are two converging tendencies that led to the cata-
clysm of Conceptual art. The first is related to society's view of art and
the second to the art itself.

Throughout the course of the twentieth century, with its catastrophic
wars, famines, population displacement, and genocide, social critics
became convinced that something was deeply wrong in Western society
and that the people in these societies needed to be awakened from their
complacent slumber. These critics believed that a self-satisfied bourgeois
existence allowed unscrupulous leaders to manipulate the populations
of their nations. They began to vehemently reject nineteenth-century
notions such as the ideas of Théophile Gaultier, whose 1834 preface to
Mademoiselle De Maupin called for removing the utilitarian and moral
purposes from art in favor of what I have been calling aesthetic values.
This Romantic creation of an art-for-art's-sake philosophy that had led
to what André Malraux called "the most profound metamorphosis,"
from utilitarian craft toward purely aesthetic creations, was viewed as
outdated if not dangerous. The artist Sarah Charlesworth has put it
this way: "When the power of validation and legitimization of human
enterprise occurs more and more within an institutionalized system,
where corporate power and investment potential are becoming increasingly the social consensus by which we signify meaning, it is clear that
no private vision, no personal vision, no personal iconoclastic gesture
can withstand."[4] So, one might say that this impossibility of personal
vision and iconoclastic gesture led to what were surely some of the
most, shall we say, idiosyncratic gestures in the history of the world.

Conceptual artists were not the first to raise this critique. Earlier
critics also questioned whether art-for-art's sake was not some sort of
opiate that the ruling classes used to stupefy and control the bourgeoisie. They just did not go quite as far. The philosopher Theodor Adorno
encouraged modern music precisely by praising its shocking and ugly
aspect. He thought that Schoenberg's ugly music was just what the
bourgeoisie needed to hear as a way of prodding them out of their com-
placency. What was "good" about the music was precisely that people

did not like it. Adorno and other modern theorists thought of art as a sort of critical mirror that would help society see its faults and jostle it into corrective action.

The best artists paid little heed to this sort of discourse. Schoenberg had no intention of writing ugly or shocking music. He sought a different kind of beauty and believed that his type of language would become so commonplace that it would be no more shocking than Mozart in a few more decades. There was such an overwhelming amount of critical discourse flowing concerning meaning and modern art that the poet Wallace Stevens quipped: "Even the lack of a reason becomes a reason. Picasso expresses surprise that people should ask what a picture means and says that pictures are not intended to have meaning. This explains everything."[5] Stevens is being facetious, but Picasso is right. The only really viable argument for art is artistic (aesthetic) and the work itself makes the argument far better than any text could. Trying to bring art or, even worse, artists into a social discourse (although we might support their social goals) is a terrible error.

If the problem had remained confined to the critical/philosophical side of the street, I suspect things would never have gotten quite so out of hand. However, artists and musicians joined in this folly, although initially their motivations and goals were quite distinct.

Though certainly not the earliest, a good example is John Cage's work (originally for the piano) from 1952 titled *4'33"*. This piece calls for a pianist to walk onstage, prepare to play with all the usual gestures, and then wait, counting off set amounts of silence. Cage has been somewhat contradictory in subsequent writings and interviews about whether he wants the audience to "listen" to the silence or to grow uncomfortable with the situation — thus calling into question aspects of the concert ritual. Extreme though this work is in some ways, it is downright traditional in others. For example, it has a written score and title; the piece takes place in a concert hall and involves a performer who has the composer's performance instructions in front of him or her; more significantly, the piece takes place in time and elicits some sort of affect from the audience (boredom or annoyance, perhaps, but affect nonetheless).

I do not believe that the intention of the early conceptually oriented works was to undermine or destroy from within the very premises on which artistic endeavor was based (as later Conceptual artists explicitly intended). The pieces, or experiments, were meant to show us the too constraining boxes we had unwittingly placed ourselves in. Many different sorts of artists felt that the weight of tradition (with the assumptions and habits that come with it) had become unbearable.

These artists responded by focusing our attention on the frame: a concert, a hall, an audience. To do this they chose to reduce the amount of aesthetic content inside the frame. In the case of *4'33"*, calling attention to the concertgoers' expectations required the complete elimination of the aesthetic object (at least one crafted and controlled by the composer) that is presented in the frame.

This was not the inevitable unfolding of a historical process. It grew out of the choices made by a small number of artists and composers with a wonderful knack for self-promotion. Even many decades earlier, other ways of addressing these same issues were possible. Impressionist painters had also been bothered by the limits of a frame. This is why many late Impressionist works have painted frames, continuing the work outside its conventional border. Seurat and others at times went so far as to paint a portion of the wall surrounding the canvas. Now, perhaps Cage felt he had to go even further, yet I believe the Impressionist example shows that the need to draw attention to the periphery and its confining assumptions does not necessarily require draining the object of its aesthetic center.

More recently, Pierre Boulez sought to call attention to another part of our inherited framework: preexisting textbook musical forms. He wrote articles, one of which famously attacks Schoenberg — the composer most directly responsible for developing the very technique of Boulez's musical language, serialism. In this article, "Schoenberg Is Dead," Boulez proclaims that Schoenberg did not go far enough in his revolution; that pouring new contents into the mold of old forms was a contradiction that was fatal to modern aesthetic aims. To promulgate his view, Boulez did not burn effigies of Schoenberg in concert halls or stage eighteenth-century-style waltz parties to Schoenberg's music where everyone wore wigs. He published his conceptual ideas as ideas presented linguistically in texts and then went home to write his music, where he hoped the aesthetic rightness of his views would become artistically evident. While Boulez felt the need to criticize and attempt to correct the past, that effort did not require sacrificing the present or the future as it did for Cage in *4'33"*. Cage would probably have disputed this characterization. He would have tried to maintain that the silence of the concert hall, or, more precisely, the random rustling sounds of the increasingly agitated audience, were real, perhaps even beautiful, "music," but I have trouble accepting that even he believed this as anything more than a useful intellectual posture.

The capital error of many artists is to assume that the issues that obsess them, in their constant absorption with their work, are necessarily the central issues of that work for outside observers. For the audience, at the moment of perception, other aspects of the work are likely to take precedence. Great art is generally balanced in a way that calls for mastery over everything from the smallest details to the largest concepts. By flattening the possible readings to a pure social critique of the existence and relevance of art — even while allowing for infinite acceptable realizations — it is the conceptual arts whose conception is "fascistic." These artists have completely divorced the ideas that might motivate an artist from the root origin of art, artisanal craft.

Until the modern, industrialized era, when we could buy nearly everything in an industrially produced, premade, ready to use form, people always made things, whether by cooking their food, fashioning their tools and utensils, or building their homes. They also made music: by singing or tapping their feet or learning to play an instrument (as used to be much more common than it is today). Some people were even very good at making some of these things. One consequence of this process of individual creation/production/fabrication has been the sort of specialization that led to systems of barter and economic exchange. Another consequence led to artisanal art. People who were able to make (or decorate) objects or music especially well could be paid by those less skillful or possessing other skills. In this way, their work could gain economic value that would allow them to spend more time on a single work. Eventually, society came to see that letting them develop these skills beyond what an individual buyer might be able to afford to subsidize could be of benefit to society as a whole. Part of the reason we could admire these particularly well-made objects in the first place, however, was our ability to empathize with the labor involved in their elaboration. I suspect that it was this sort of projection (imagining the amount of effort) that first helped people separate the ideas of taste and value. With an object whose elaboration we can empathize with it is relatively easy to say, "I don't like the style, but can you imagine how difficult and time consuming this must have been to make?"

These artisanal origins can still be seen all over the vocabulary and structure of the art world. Even the notion of a masterpiece is an outgrowth of artisanal work. A masterpiece was just that: a master's piece. Within the corporate structure of crafts, artisans worked under contract for a specified period of time as an apprentice. Then the artisan spent an unspecified period of time as a journeyman. When a craftsman was ready to settle and open a proper workshop where he (only men were allowed) could have his own apprentices, he had to convince the appropriate local craft corporation to admit him as a master. The two aspects to be adjudicated prior to his acceptance were the craftsman's financial viability (measured by his ability to pay a hefty professional tax) and his skill, which was demonstrated by producing a master's piece. This masterpiece became the property of the craft corporation (these corporations were very similar to the guilds that operated in some parts of Europe, but were a bit less restrictive) and established the artisan's high level of professional competence.

Craft corporations used the word "masterpiece" in this way since the Middle Ages; it was during the sixteenth century that the broader notion of an "absolute" masterpiece entered artistic discourse. At this point, the idea that a (absolute) masterpiece had a sort of perfection became current. In 1669, the sculptor Gaspard Marsy spoke of a sculpture as being an inimitable masterpiece whose origin was more divine than human. It took the creation of public expositions, then museums (the Louvre opened to the public in 1793) for the modern and romantic notion of the masterpiece to be complete in the minds of the general public.[6]

While no one disputes this link between artisanal craft and art's past, since we now live in the industrial (or perhaps postindustrial) era, many see no reason to maintain that link in art's future. I wrote in Chapter 2 about the changes that Max Weber felt broke the previously unified hierarchical view of society into separate domains of knowledge and expertise. This separation gave artists greater freedom, not just to perfect their craft but also to choose at least some of the ends to which that craft was directed. Concepts and ideas could drive their creations and become an important ingredient in ways that were much broader than had been possible when works had to correspond to rigid categories or be highly functional. I would argue, however, that really great art can only happen in this way, when craft and concept are married in the realization of aesthetic objects. By keeping art attached in some way to its artisanal past, by at least preserving a made object, audiences can still develop the sort of empathy that allows them to imagine themselves in the place of the creator. This empathy allows them to interact personally, not remotely and abstractly, with the object (and a piece of music is also an object in this sense) in a way that can engage their aesthetic sense.

With the rise of industrialization, however, both artists and their audiences think much less about craft when they appreciate objects. So few of the things around us are actually directly made by an individual. Much more important to our contemporary view of an object is its function (What does it do?). How most modern devices work or how they were made may be hopelessly beyond the usual learning abilities of even highly educated individuals. In this context, it is not surprising that many artists would begin to feel that what their art does is more important than what it is or how it was made. This is the central preoccupation of conceptual art: What does art do? If that is their guiding principle, it is no wonder that they were ready to destroy art if its effects (what it does) were detrimental to society.

But, as I said before, Picasso had the right idea. Art *is* different: It doesn't really have a function in that sense. This can be puzzling because we have made our lives so function oriented, but art doesn't really do or mean anything other than what it is (as an object) and perhaps what it does on purely aesthetic terms. Oscar Wilde quipped, "All bad poetry is sincere," and I think the larger truth to his quip is that the more art tries to be about or for important, extra-aesthetic (especially political) things, the weaker it tends to be artistically. In the final paragraph of her essay "How One Should Read a Book," Virginia Woolf wrote of her aesthetic pleasure in reading: "Are there not some pursuits that we practice because they are good in themselves, and some pleasures that are final? And is this not among them?" I think it is ridiculous to accept the Marxist critique that creating wondrous aesthetic objects can somehow help fascist regimes by anesthetizing the bourgeoisie into tolerating their most heinous acts. What I believe aesthetic objects can do, however, is improve the existence of some individuals, regardless of the regimes under which they must live. The great error of all Marxist reasoning is granting the individual so little voice; Marxists call for an existence with the diversions of entertainment but not the joy of art.

It may be a primitive sensation, but the ability to appreciate an aesthetically formed thing — whether visual, aural, linguistic, or physical — is a remarkable experience, one that lets us empathize across time and culture. Moreover, creating and appreciating aesthetic objects shaped by our hands and minds are part of our identity as human beings. The skills and techniques developed over millennia have allowed us to create remarkable things. These objects are often far more awe-inspiring than the many technical wonders of modern life, because there is still that empathic echo that lets the receiver imagine himself in the role of creator, discovering or imagining the intentions of that creator. Though that link can survive a great deal of stretching, once it is completely severed, when an object no longer feels created or no longer exists — and no sense of human thought or hands can be sensed — then Buren is indeed right: "Art is no longer there. It's about something else." Once there is no aesthetic value, what remains is, at most, a limited sort of philosophy.

4
ELITISM

Gradually and reluctantly, however, I realized that the wrath directed at elitism has less to do with money than with [...] scorn for the very kinds of intellectual distinction-making I hold most dear: [...] upholding of objective standards; most important, the willingness to assert unyieldingly that one idea, contribution or attainment is better than another. The worst aspect of what gets called "political correctness" these days is the erosion of intellectual confidence needed to sort out, and rank, competing values. It used to be that intellectual debate centered on the results of such an assessment. We have retrenched to the point that the very act of starting the process requires audacity ...

— **William A. Henry, III**[1]

In the late 1980s, I attended the Peabody Conservatory in Baltimore, where I studied musical composition. Once a week all the composition students took a seminar along with the composition faculty. Guests were sometimes invited, but the main purpose of the meetings was for students to present their works. Most composition programs offer something like this seminar, but never have I seen one reach the level of aggression, meanness, and almost brutality of these meetings.

Just prior to my enrollment as a student at Peabody, a group of four students had so terrorized their colleagues at these seminars that they became known as "the gang of four." This shark-pit/feeding-frenzylike atmosphere is hardly the norm for composition seminars. In fact, in the equivalent seminar at Columbia, I can remember almost the whole student body rallying around colleagues who received even mild criticisms. (I have been back to Peabody's composition seminar in recent years, and while the discussions are still lively, the environment there, too, has become more civil.) While I can certainly think of many problems that grew out of this incredibly confrontational atmosphere (and it certainly felt awful the first few times you were publicly ripped to shreds), sometimes this environment made it possible to speak a truth that usually remains unsaid.

At one particular session a composer presented a long, slow work during which very little happened and the things that did happen were not very interesting. The sharks, smelling blood in the water, began to circle (the atmosphere tended to get more and more charged the worse the piece being presented was thought to be by the seminar participants). The comments began with gentle probing, dancing around the surely fatal attack we all wanted to make: "The piece is boring." This particular composer was not some naïve freshman who would breakdown in tears and leave, however (as I'm ashamed to say happened several times); he was prepared to fight back. The composer began to explain his work. He stressed that he was trying to achieve a sort of stasis, a lack of happening, and then he pulled out the ultimate trump card. He said, "I really wanted to create an effect of boredom — music is too much about things happening; I wanted you to feel like there's nothing; I wanted the listener to feel bored and restless." This, of course, suddenly turned the whole debate on its head. Now, if someone said, "Your piece was boring," the composer could respond, "Thank you — that's just what I was going for." Our best weapon now blunted, we discussed, for some time in a fairly civil manner, how one might evoke the notion of boredom without actually inducing the sensation of boredom. But, no — he wanted to bore us. He was adamant about this, no half measures or analogies: we were meant to be nodding off. Finally, Robert Hall Lewis, one of the professors known for his outrageous and very politically incorrect statements, raised his hand and said, "Just because you have an idea and you realize that idea, does not mean it is a good idea and certainly does not mean it is a good piece."

Readers who have persevered to this point are probably willing to concede that some pieces of music are better than others in at least some way. However, once we stop thinking of a piece as the disembodied artwork of an anonymous human being, but as the personal creation of an individual person, things get much harder. If we could believe that the differences were simply a reflection of differing degrees of skill, we might be all right. It seems fairly acceptable to assert that some people have more skill than others at particular tasks, but this is certainly not enough to explain why some works and, more troublingly, some ideas seem better than others. Great art seems to be the result of someone having the right ideas for his or her particular set of skills. Or perhaps it comes from having great ideas and at least sufficient craft to realize those ideas.

A well-known anecdote involves the composers Hector Berlioz (1803–1869) and Camille Saint-Saëns (1835–1921). Saint-Saëns was a remarkable prodigy, even in comparison to others like Mozart. It was said that you could name any piece from the entire history of music and he could go to the piano and play it, not just the main theme but the whole thing. (I suspect this reputation must have been at least a little exaggerated, but the feat is astounding nonetheless.) In concert he let the audience chose any of the Beethoven sonatas for him to play from memory. Saint-Saëns must have been thoroughly familiar with thousands of works. Late in his life when he had become an acknowledged leader among the so-called "advanced" composers, Berlioz was asked for his opinion about Saint-Saëns, and he replied that there's not much you can say about Saint-Saëns, since he knows everything. He ventured, however, that the one thing Saint-Saëns might lack was a bit of ignorance (sometimes the term used in the anecdote is "inexperience"). For all his incredible knowledge, skill, and talent, Saint-Saëns's ideas were only mediocre. He lacked the imagination, ambition, or ability to reach beyond the vast reservoir of his knowledge and strive for something truly new or personal. Saint-Saëns unquestionably knew what he wanted to say and was able to say it with great skill. Yet, his music does not have the same power or impact as the best works of a composer like Berlioz, whose technical skills were only middling.

By now you're probably wondering what these anecdotes have to do with elitism. The word "elitism" itself has become a terrible condemnation. Calling someone an elitist is only slightly better than calling him or her a racist or a bigot. It has come to imply disdain, or at least a lack of respect and understanding for the value of everyone and everything outside of the elite to which one is said to belong. History, of course, gives us ample historical reason for mistrusting any group that holds itself above others. So many of these groups have based their supposed superiority on criteria that most of us would judge to be at best invalid and at worst immoral (racial superiority, gender superiority, divine right, hereditary position, etc.). If one is to be fair, however, most of these repugnant elites were drawn from societies whose dominant views were almost equally distasteful.

Sociological discussions of elitism, especially those prevalent prior to World War II, and found even in Aristotle, did not build their arguments around whether there ought to be elites or whether valid criteria (absolute or political) existed for forming elites. The authors' ideas resulted from observations of human societies and organizations that all contained some sort of elite. That elites reflect realities in human life is as true today as it was in 1896 when the sociologist Gaetano Mosca published his *Elementi di Scienza Politica*:

> We all know that, in our own country, whichever it may be, the management of public affairs is in the hands of a minority of influential persons, to which management, willingly or unwillingly, the majority defer. We know the same thing goes on in neighboring countries, and in fact we should be put to it to conceive of a real world otherwise organized — a world in which men would be directly subject to a single person without relationships of subordination, or in which all men would share equally in the direction of political affairs.[2]

Moreover, at least in the realm of politics, most of us accept these elites perfectly willingly as long as they seem to be chosen either by the majority (democratically) or upon some evident system of merit (meritocratically). At times we are even willing to accept the idea that a bad elite could, under certain circumstances, be preferable to no elite. Look at the system of referenda in California, which is so often criticized.

Here is what we should all be seeking: a truly egalitarian system of governance. Yet the result is anything but felicitous. Referenda allow majorities to state their will without having to reconcile the conflicts inherent in their desires. Thus it is easy to vote for increased services although they come at a higher cost, then place a cap on spending because government is wasteful, and finally top it all off with a vote to decrease revenue through tax cuts — and we have three desires whose admixture is ruinous. Any party that openly tries to achieve all three goals at the same time would appear ridiculous, but in a referendum the responsibility is so diffuse that the ensuing mess feels more like an act of fate than a fault of governance. Any actual elite eventually bears the consequences of its decisions (though it may cause enormous harm and suffering first). The paradox, though, is that in spite of our clear acceptance of elites, even in spite of the fact that nearly all of us are constantly jockeying for position within one hierarchy or another, the word "elitism" has become an epithet — why?

I think the quote that opens this chapter, from an otherwise disturbing volume (the author's main goal is to rail against affirmative action and to lobby for wealth as the true measure of worth), gets at part of the answer. We have come to believe that while some hierarchies may be necessary, they are never fully legitimate — they always represent biases and distortions. This essentially correct notion has sometimes led us to the opposite extreme, which I think is at least as wrong as blind faith in authority. Too often people have come to believe that all hierarchies are completely illegitimate. I don't wish to rehash the arguments in favor of absolute values and criteria from earlier chapters, but we do need to look at the benefit all of us might reap from an unequal distribution of resources. In other words, a completely egalitarian distribution of resources might not be in the interests of the vast majority, even of some of those who would have more under that system.

In the domains of politics and economics, most of us have accepted the idea that a fully egalitarian approach does not work. Without going into a detailed review of the complexities of Cold War politics, it seems clear from the ruinous and inegalitarian results of so many attempts to create communist societies and the needs of even small-scale communes to adopt a leadership structure that a completely egalitarian division of wealth, power, and responsibility is incompatible with human psychology. We need incentives, hopes, at least an illusion of progress. It is very difficult to imagine a human society where everyone would receive the same salary, spend the same number of hours a day on work and leisure, have identical levels of education and responsibility, and so on. Even if everyone had identical abilities, their inclinations would still be varied.

In modern societies, we try to create a mixture, where certain minima are guaranteed to all. While on the upper end we don't necessarily directly limit the accumulation of wealth, some societies do tax wealth directly, and most tax inheritances (cross-generational accumulation). A progressive income tax structure — used in some form by most nations — is also an attempt to redistribute wealth from upper incomes to lower incomes. Even foreign aid of various sorts is a sort of transnational redistribution of wealth from richer countries to poorer ones whose aim is presumably to promote more equality, social justice, or at least social stability — although no nation ships enough of its gross domestic product abroad to eliminate the enormous imbalances between rich and poor nations.

In fields like education, we adopt a similar system where societies determine minimal amounts of schooling (for example, until age sixteen) required for all, while permitting a subset of the population to invest a larger portion of their lives in pursuit of further studies; the more years of studies, the smaller the fraction of the population to which it can be offered. Similar criteria apply to the performing arts: Everyone can be in his or her first grade pageant or junior high talent show, but very few can star on Broadway.

On purely empirical grounds, it does not seem that we have a fundamental problem with inequality. For me personally, the problem is not elites based on merit, but elites of birth, gender, race, or class. I suspect that for many people, however, the acceptance or rejection of an elite is based not on a sense of social justice, but on one of two conditions. The first is a belief that it might be possible (even if unlikely) to one day join that elite. This is why politicians who come from the most charmed backgrounds still pretend to be regular Joes, allowing us to think, "If he could do it, so could I or my child." We also accept elites whose membership requires special qualifications that most of us cannot even delude ourselves into believing we will ever possess. We must believe society as a whole will benefit in some way from the output of these elites and that the criteria for membership in the elite have at least some validity (e.g., medical research). The arts used to be more like this latter type of elite, although the cult of celebrity has made at least some art forms into something more like the former.

Of course, these two justifications for elites (lotto winners and highly trained benefactors, if you like) leave someone like a contemporary art-music composer in a terrible bind. While I believe that most people do not feel they could ever do the work of a composer, they are far from sure that there is any benefit to them from the work these composers do. Many are also probably unsure whether these "artists" have any real skills at all and must wonder whether they are simply charlatans. Perhaps the only value (utility, benefit) that most of society is still willing to grant to even the most esoteric art-forms is its usefulness as self-expression, which is thought to be a good thing (at least in the abstract) and which is certainly a right guaranteed by the First Amendment. Unfortunately, this creates a new problem.

Although we tolerate grave inequities in many domains, especially quantitative ones, we have come to demand at least a semblance of equity in the domains of human and civil rights. We expect at least the pretense of equal justice under law; we expect medical care to be available to all (or at least are briefly outraged when reminded that it is not); and if we have come to view art as first and foremost self-expression, how can we possibly accept some "selves" as being more worthy of being expressed? This is a sort of elitism that seems completely intolerable.

As I mentioned earlier, we might avoid this problem by defending artistic elitism based on a notion of craftsmanship, but that just doesn't work in a post-Conceptual art era because almost no one would now claim that greater craft leads automatically to greater art. Even in earlier eras, the exact correlation between craft and art is not linear (as the Berlioz comments about Saint-Saëns point out). I think that most people would still recognize that the level of skill required to make most art of whatever type requires intense and (from society's viewpoint) expensive training. It seems clear that this training cannot be made freely available to all comers without posing a burden that society would never be willing to bear. Moreover, an art like contemporary classical music is doubly burdensome. Composers don't produce wealth as they become more successful; they consume it. Bigger, more prominent events lose even more money (and require more subsidies) than small student concerts. The success of a composer can be measured by taking the inverse of the composer's market value: The more negative the market value, the more important the composer.

Self-expression is a domain where assessments like right or wrong, better or worse, are not considered appropriate. Therefore no elitist-type judgments can be made. From this point of view, Robert Hall Lewis had no right to tell that student that his idea was bad or consequently that the piece was bad. It belonged to that individual and expressed something he felt. That composer already knew the power of this attitude — the power of saying, "That was my intent." In a less contentious environment than those campus seminars, this viewpoint will nearly always end all possible argument. It's permissible to discuss whether someone has achieved his or her aims, but not the legitimacy of those aims. Debating the validity (or interest) of someone's intentions has become "elitist."

Evaluating the legitimacy of any type of self-expression has become somewhat hopeless. You can never be sure you're right, so most will not even try. I once asked one of my teachers what he would say to a composer he thought had no chance of becoming a good or even adequate composer. He responded by recounting a well-known story told by the composer John Cage in *Conversing with Cage*. When Cage studied briefly with the renowned modernist and inventor of twelve-tone composition, Arnold Schoenberg, Schoenberg apparently became very frustrated with Cage's work one day and said to him, "You have no ear for harmony and no sense of melody or rhythm; if you stay in composition you will only be banging your head against the wall." To which Cage says he replied, "In that case I would devote my life to beating my head against that wall." This story offers a glimpse of one of the greatest composition teachers of the twentieth century seen through the eyes of perhaps his most "untrainable" student, and even in this extreme case Schoenberg could not be sure whose ideas would turn out to be important. Some might even argue that Cage is the most influential composer to have studied with Schoenberg.

If we accept this idea that even the most skilled teacher cannot always differentiate among the validity of individual approaches, we are trapped in two different ways. First, a composition teacher can't really help any students he or she might find particularly worthy, because this would be unfair to the others who are *a priori* equally worthy. Second, it is very hard to try to convince and educate a public to see the worth in works if we adopt a view of art so focused on the self of the artist. This attitude requires the transformation of art appreciation into a form of spectator psychoanalysis — an approach that is widely in use by a segment of art critics. So how can we avoid these traps without reasserting some, clearly false, notion of composer infallibility?

We must first try to deflate the myth that art is self-expression. Art is both expressive and personal, but, especially with an abstract art like music, it is much more than (and somewhat less than) self-expression. Another former teacher of mine told the following parable (composition teachers, myself included, are very fond of telling stories):

> One summer three composers fall madly in love. All three of them independently decide to express their feelings in the form of a love duet for oboe d'amore and cello. The first is more in love than anyone has ever been in the history of the human race. The second, while only normally in love, is more sensitive and self-aware about his feelings of love than anyone has ever been. The third composer on the other hand is a bit of a cold-fish. While she is somewhat infatuated, it is quite superficial and not very important (this composer is already planning on how to break it off in a week or two). However this person is by far the best composer. Whose piece will be the most beautiful, most moving, most expressive of love? Without a doubt it would be the third composer.

It seems cosmically unjust, but there is nothing special about the humanity of artists. What is special is their artistry — nothing more or less. If your goal were to know love, a date would have a greater chance of success than a work of art. Art is a special substance into which some individuals are able to transform life through a poorly understood alchemical process. If we even *partially* accept this notion that artists' humanity is not special and what we are engaging with is not their self, but a work; if we accept that even the greatest artists are not special people, but people who make special things; then we can remove the second obstacle I mentioned. These are not narrowly focused pieces of introspection, but potentially meaningful exteriorizations.

The first problem — fairness — remains, however, because we cannot be sure of our judgments: How can we single out one person to whom we will give an opportunity and ignore another? I have suggested in previous chapters that there might be legitimate criteria for making these choices, yet you will have noticed that I am not going to suggest exactly what they are. These criteria — if they exist — reflect deep and sometimes contradictory aspects of the way we perceive. Moreover, any insight about these criteria we might possess will be filtered by our culture and experience. I suspect that, like the position and velocity vector of a subatomic particle, we can never achieve more than a working approximation that will always be somewhat stochastic in nature. In Chapters 7, 8, and 9, I will try to look more closely at the kind of mental representations that must be involved in creating these criteria. For now, I would like to suggest that even if we use the wrong criteria or make the wrong choices, an erroneous or random selection still might be better than not making any choices. I believe that giving resources even to the "wrong" artists would still be better than an egalitarian system that gives almost nothing to almost everyone.

If we choose a select few to train and even fewer to disseminate to the public, we will undoubtedly make choices that are less than perfect. Our biases and tastes will interfere with even the most well-intentioned efforts to evaluate the potential of creators and the worth of works. Moreover, there may well be different frameworks, styles, or idioms for evaluating these works and creators and the evaluations yielded may be incompatible. Sometimes the evaluators may be corrupt, sometimes they may be flat-out wrong, but making these choices, right or wrong, will do something wonderful: It will open to those selected individuals (worthy or not) enormous possibilities to freely explore their artistic abilities. You might say, "Sure that's wonderful for them, but what does it do for the rest of us? Surely society cannot be expected to do this for very many individuals, so what's the point?" However, by granting this opportunity to even a few individuals, all of us will benefit.

The first thing that happens is that we can compare the works these artists produce. In this way, we begin to establish a context. We start to see what people are capable of freed from most of the constraints that are normally present. Moreover, these works allow us to consider the criteria for judgment we used in selecting these creators and works in the first place. Once a system and a context exist, it is easy to improve them. Building this system from scratch is a monumental task, however: It is like compiling the first dictionary. Even in periods when the link between audience and artist is weakened and we wonder whether the results of most working artists are worthwhile, it would be tragic to risk the entire system that allows artists to be trained and works to be created. Think of what it takes to create a new opera: an opera composer, an orchestra, set designers, singers, and so on. The apparatus reaches all the way from a neighborhood piano teacher through conservatories like Juilliard or Peabody to the great opera houses. The amount of societal infrastructure that allows the Metropolitan Opera to put on the occasional new opera is mind-boggling. Even if *most* of these operas are truly awful (although more likely they will just be mediocre), none would be possible without this apparatus.

This is not to say that the public should sit back and passively accept whatever art an "elite" offers them. The advantage of having works produced and offered is that it gives us the best possible tool for really evaluating and comparing them. We may decide that everything at the Whitney Biennial is awful, but events like this give us the chance to judge a few works and consider some ideas in an enormously idealized situation where we can engage with the work on as close to purely aesthetic terms as possible. Perhaps equally important, new generations of artists can interact with these works and a few of them will use their experiences as a background for refining their own still inchoate ideas.

As long as traditions and institutions don't become an absolute barrier against change or openness to innovation, their presence provides an enormous service. The cost of maintaining this system once it exists is orders of magnitude less than the cost of building it initially. Therefore, allowing that infrastructure to wither during artistic low points poses the great risk of not having the conditions necessary for the next renaissance. If we have a canon, it is easy to debate what should be included within it. If we do not attempt to make those choices and limit our horizon constructively, however, I fear that almost everything will drown in an undifferentiated flood of work. It would be wonderful to discern faultlessly the most meretricious works, to have a truly meritocratic elite that represents the best from all domains using various and complementary criteria. However, until we can be sure we have achieved that perfect standard of judgment, I think society as a whole benefits more from our honest attempts at creating an approximation of that ideal. As long as we are on the lookout for ways to improve our approximation, we gain nothing and lose much by demanding perfection before accepting a flawed compromise; we run the risk of ending up with nothing.

Something that often surprises the friends and families of composers is that we don't spend much time listening to music recreationally. Some composers I know don't even like most other people's music (even that of the greats). We don't become composers because we see this amazing thing and want to do the same; we become composers because we think something is not being done or is being done wrong. I think many, if not most of us, believe that we are the only ones who see something that needs to be different. Nietzsche spoke of creation as a form of mental illness. He said anyone really sane would be content with what already exists. For those of us with this disease, we are willing to spend as much time in training as a brain surgeon, and work for wages that are sometimes lower than the custodial staff that cleans the hall after the concert, so that we might have the opportunity to figure out what we believe is wrong with the works out there and how to fix it. Most of us may be wrong, but if even a few of us are on to something, and if even a few of those few are given the chance to develop their skills, and if even a few members of that much smaller group have the chance to use their skills to make works that can cause all of us to reassess how we see or hear, it seems amply worth the cost.

5

TECHNOLOGY

By its nature, interactive technology will also offer a wealth of choices about how a story unfolds, so no two people's entertainment experience need ever be the same. Writers will not have to script entire tales ahead of time, because the people who enter the story will become the characters whose decisions move the story along. A writer may shape the initial circumstances, but the story will unfold improvisationally. The story environment — and characters within it — will respond to personal messages, news and other forms of information. What this kind of virtual storyworld will require is a database network that is embedded with enough story elements and decision-making algorithms to generate various serendipitous actions with unique content.

— Glorianna Davenport[1]

Some have turned to new technology as a possible savior for the ills faced by contemporary art. Certainly, technological innovations in computers and digitization have revolutionized many areas of our lives. Industrial development has taught us that things will continually get better, smaller, faster — whether we need them to or not. Often, new technology seems to be created simply because it is possible. Often we must just scratch our heads and wonder about some new technology's usefulness until someone comes along with that "killer app" that makes us wonder how we lived without it. However, the possibility that a transformative application of the technology *might* be possible is not, in and of itself, a justification for confidence that technology can cure the ills afflicting artistic domains. For many years some have offered as the defense for mediocre works (both artistic and commercial) employing technology the underdeveloped state of the technology. Developers and artists say, "Just wait, when the computers or software get a little better, this will really be something." It is hard to believe this could be the real problem, however.

Look at the history of musical instrument design: Every stage of its technological development saw wondrous works written for whatever instruments were available. We went from hard-to-tune keyboards with no dynamic range to the technological wonder of a modern concert grand, yet a generation of composers never existed who said, "Our music for keyboard instruments would be great if only we had dynamics, or better temperaments, and so on." We still admire pieces written for all stages in the development of these instruments. In fact, one of the great ironies of music is that Bach's *Well-Tempered Clavier* is often presented in music appreciation classes as requiring and helping to promote the emergence of our modern tuning system of "equal temperament."[2] I have even heard it suggested that these pieces were the "killer app." convincing the world that equal temperament was needed. The pieces were not written for equal temperament, however, and I suspect that given the choice Bach would not have wanted a performer to use this "more perfect temperament."

The idea of equal temperament is that, as far as possible, all keys should sound alike (in practice they must all be a little, but only a little, out of tune). Mistaken music appreciation teachers will say that Bach needed this temperament to be free to modulate to distant keys. However, prior to the development of truly equal temperament there were many systems of achieving "well-tempered" music. These tunings would allow one to play in any key (unlike earlier mean-tone temperaments, for example, which would only make usable a small subset of the keys, while leaving the others too far out of tune for use). These well-temperaments, however, left the various keys very dissimilar. Some were extremely out of tune and tense, barely playable, while others boasted the almost perfectly in-tune thirds[3] that equal temperament so sorely lacks. With a well-tempered clavier, modulations are not just movements from one key to another; they are huge transformations of the color of the instrument: pure to gritty, stable to wobbling, and so on. An important reason for writing in all keys (besides the obvious pedagogical reasons) was to show how different they were, not to exploit their homogeneity.

To take a more general example, the instruments used in a modern orchestra have changed tremendously since even the late-nineteenth century. Yet Beethoven, Mozart, and Haydn seemed able to come up with awfully good pieces in spite of the technical deficiencies of their technology (poorly tuned woodwinds, brass with limited agility, etc.). A major trend of the last couple of decades has even been to use these less-developed instruments to play more "historically accurate" versions of the pieces. These recordings are often more popular and more critically admired than recordings that are more technically perfect (more in tune, better balanced, greater range of instrumental timbre, etc.). This is not different from other domains, even technological ones. A major movement in video games in the last few years has been retro. Software simulations of early arcade and Atari video games are now available. There is no question that new games offer a greater palette of graphical and interface possibilities, but that doesn't mean that they will be more fun or engaging. The success of a work depends on how it uses its medium, not on the absolute sophistication of that medium.

Caveats aside, though, we should still consider whether there might be a technological cure for many of the problems we've been discussing. Could technology, in and of itself, heal the division between artist and audience? Perhaps the difficulties lie not with aesthetics or values, but with an aging media. Maybe the medium *is* the message, and it is not the art music that turns people off but the concert hall. Perhaps too often the music itself does not take sufficient advantage of the technological possibilities now available. Bach used the most up-to-date technology available to him (especially in the domain of organs), and while his works don't suffer from advances not yet developed, perhaps we would feel differently if he had turned his back on "modern advances" and written only for Renaissance instruments.

As I see it, there are two ways in which technology could make a real impact on the kind of nonfunctional art we've been discussing and both of them already are being actively explored. First, technological innovations could facilitate many things that are not new. They might make existing processes better or cheaper in ways that might alter the situation meaningfully. For example, we might all be able to make the kind of total multimedia art experience Wagner dreamed of a reality — and we could do it without getting a government to build a special theater and fund a festival (though our grandchildren might need to look for work if we skipped those steps). Wagner had been inspired to move in this direction by the last movement of Beethoven's Ninth Symphony and he had the clout, talent, and acumen to accomplish a large part of his goals. When Scriabin (a much less forceful politician), however, wanted to take the ideas even further using massive mechanical and human resources, it was impossible. Technology might change all of that. We could reach far-flung virtual audiences and perhaps render viable art that could not command enough of a public in any one city or country. Moreover, we may need these new facilities to replace the vanishing infrastructure of publishers, orchestras that play new works, stores that stock new works (or even more generally classical music) in score or recording form, and so on.

The second way technology could change art is through the more profound revision of the role of artist and art-perceiver, as noted by the MIT Media Lab researcher Glorianna Davenport. Perhaps entirely new ways of imagining and creating art exist now. Some might even say that better, more engaging kinds of art can now be created. Perhaps we have alienated audiences because they will no longer accept the largely passive role of art-perceiver; they want to be an art-shaper as well. Saying that they must actively listen and that their perception shapes the work might not cut it any more in our brave new world. Maybe what art needs is more interactivity.

I'd like to discuss these two potential applications of technology to art separately, at least initially. Before we accept these technological panaceas, we need to look at the potential artistic cost that could come from adopting these technologies. Let's start with the second situation. I have heard many artists argue that this is the future. Some feel that user-shaped environments are somehow more engaging, more demo-cratic, potentially more meaningful to the individual viewer. Moreover, many have claimed that this kind of work is more in tune with the everything-at-the-same-time quality of contemporary life.

Imagine that you received a commission to create an interactive environment for a church. The church walls are already decorated, but you can use all the space above the windows. The idea is to convey not just one or two subjects but a whole panorama of Christian iconog-raphy. You need to include images of thirty-three separate ancestors of Jesus as well as twelve different oracles and prophets. The central images to be framed by these figures will be three sets of three images depicting the creation of the world, the creation and fall of man, and the story of Noah. Because congregants want to be able to use the space for services and don't want to obscure the artwork already in place, you can't hang any screens downward, but you can cover the ceiling with projected images. Perhaps you could convince the congregation to put some sensors on the floor, but high volumes of visitors are expected, so you will only have limited ability to tailor the experience to each person who enters. You can certainly divide up the territory and have many images going at one time. In addition, you might make some images bigger than others to create a perceptual gradient to the dif-ferent narratives. Perhaps you could measure the density of people in the room and when more congregated in one section you would favor the creation of the world (perhaps near the entry); when people were congregating near the altar you might concentrate on the creation and fall of Man. Perhaps the Noah scene would be triggered by a humidity sensor on the roof (detecting when it was raining). One can imagine that viewers coming in to see the installation might go to considerable efforts to see "what it will do." They may try to trigger the sensors in various ways to solicit different permutations. They may even try to stay long enough to have seen most or all of the variants.

These congregants may be deeply engaged, but my fear is that two crucial things will have been lost, which both contribute so strongly to the effectiveness of the noninteractive version of this site-specific installation. First, we might lose our ability to appreciate the thing that is there in front of or above us. I fear that when we try to manipulate and control something it is harder, if not impossible, to observe and perceive it in a deep way. Think about the difference between really watching a fire crackle and burn and using a bellows to try to keep the fire going. In both cases you see the fire, but in the second case your vision is largely quantitative and utilitarian: How big are the flames? Are things getting hotter or not? When staring into a fire, however, we appreciate it qualitatively and make aesthetic, not utilitarian, judgments: It is beautiful or fascinating. I fear that these may be highly distinct cognitive systems; in which case real aesthetic appreciation would to a certain extent require the freeing of cognitive resources offered by some degree of passivity. It might certainly require the disengagement of the problem-solving sort of attitude we often engage in active tasks. (I think this is why many professional musicians describe a sort of professional deformation that forces them to analyze whatever they hear in an active manner, which can diminish the visceral aesthetic appreciation.)

The second potential loss comes from the diminished sense of the artists' agency within the work. I have criticized previously the idea that a work of art is a direct form of expression or communication, highlighting instead the as-if communication that comes from our empathic link to a creator. Even the most puzzling features will be assumed to have some sort of as-if meaning. And while it will be impossible to decode the actual artist's intentions (and some features may, from the artist's viewpoint, have been unintentional accidents), the effort to decode a sort of as-if, imagined, intention will lead us to a deeper and perhaps more meaningful (to us) reading of the work. In a famous psychology experiment viewers see geometric objects moving randomly on a television screen as directed agents with purpose and even personality; so, too, do many cultures and most young children attach agency to the seasons or the weather. However, if I raise my hand, triggering a motion detector that causes something to appear, I am the agent and I know why I lifted that arm: to see what would happen. The magical quality of trying to intuit meaning may be greatly lessened. I might wonder why the artist associated that image with a raised hand, but my reading may well stop at the level of why link gesture x to result y. If I am reading a complex multifaceted individual creation, however, I may be inclined to go further and read into how the placement and execution of the image should impact my reading not just of that choice but of that choice's effect on the object. Even in the case of work with a much lesser degree of richness (say an all-blue canvas of Yves Klein), I will be forced to ask why he would stay with a single color, how his reading of art history led to this. If placing my foot in a certain square turns the ceiling blue, I'm not sure that I would take my attribution process as far; I would be more inclined to see how it changes if I move to another area.

These two problems are from the viewpoint of the receiver; I fear that other problems may enter if we look at the situation from the artist's perspective. Although Davenport is right that richness and complexity can be generated with "a database network that is embedded with enough story elements and decision-making algorithms to generate various serendipitous actions with unique content," I'm not sure how easy or even possible it might be to make great art this way. Many great novels have great characters, but great characters are surely not sufficient to ensure their quality. Likewise interesting situations or types of interactional ground rules may be fascinating, but I fear they are more likely to generate an infinitude of so-so works rather the singularly remarkable work that is art's essential contribution.

Interactive environments are by their nature approximate (some might say flexible), making it difficult to present a strongly personal result. You might argue that I am making an error, because in these new types of works the singular artist is not the creator of the environment, but the amalgam of that creator plus the creative input of the perceiver. While I cannot absolutely deny the possibility of a team effort producing something special, I am highly skeptical. Artists, for good or ill, invest heavily of their time, thoughts, and ideas in a work, whereas viewers are necessarily coming in only at the end. Their contributions can only have a limited amount of artistic control or planning. In most cases, viewers need some time just to figure out what different actions accomplish, so their attempts to control the action will be ad hoc. This kind of interaction captures the improvised nature of life, but lacks the pseudo-improvised, but actually controlled artifice of so much great art. Moreover, art has always served to give us feelings, ideas, and sounds that change us, and this is difficult to accomplish while we are in control. We achieve these states by submitting to the artist and trying to decipher his or her meaning, not by controlling them ourselves. Religious individuals do not achieve a worshipful state by being God, we achieve it by contemplating God's actions (or the actions we attribute to a God).

Let's return to the commission for a site-specific religious installation and see what an actual artist decided to do. The actual commission was awarded in 1508, so Michelangelo Buonarroti had no computers or projection screens available. Thus interactivity was not an option. He faced some technological issues, however. He was not very familiar with fresco techniques, and their use in such a large-scale work was particularly problematic, but he sought advice and learned the necessary techniques. The more profound problem was how to order the quantity of images he wanted to include while still creating a comprehensible overall structure. His solution was to make use of image size and placement. In the lunettes and spandrels along the lateral wall, he placed the ancestors of Jesus. In the space between these ancestors, he placed the prophets and oracles. Together all these figures create a frame for the central story images that run down the center of the ceiling (both a pictorial and a theological frame). The nine story images are divided into three triptychs, beginning at one end with the most cosmological, the separation of Light and Darkness and leading across to the most human, the Drunkenness of Noah. Michelangelo painted arches across the ceiling to delineate these nine pictorial fields. Yet in the clutter of images, another level of hierarchy was desired. From the nine images, the four placed over the spandrels were made larger, the other five smaller. The five smaller framing works and the prophets/oracles below them were decorated to appear as wide framing pillars around the four, now highlighted, works: The Creation of Sun and Moon, The Creation of Adam, The Fall and the Expulsion from Paradise, and The Flood. Thus the three three-part story lines are combined into a single four-part story that tells of the creation of the world in which we live. This vast number of items is now arranged to allow readings at levels of hierarchy stretching from the unitary decorative conception through three levels of theological and artistic separations down to the individual panels, which are all multifaceted in and of themselves.

Although it is possible to imagine other combinations of these elements, which might perhaps be equally full of both aesthetic and conceptual meaning, the sheer detail of the choices allows us to feel that the arrangement is meaningful. A more mobile form might be equally beautiful, at least in some configurations, but I fear we would lose the essential illusion that we are seeing something through someone else's eyes. Even if the ever-shifting slideshow of images hit on exactly the configuration of images that currently exist, would we really read so much into the hierarchical arrangement, especially if we knew that a new arrangement was only minutes away?

Peter Weibel, one of the main artists behind Austria's Ars Electronica festival and prize, stated the case for interactivity this way:

> I realized that this is in fact the point of electronic media. In the natural world we have the illusion of being external observers; when touching something it appears not to change. But in the electronic media the basic principle is interactivity. Even a painting, like a star, exists when not being watched, but you have to put a videocassette into a recorder to watch it. This is the lowest degree of interactivity. All these multimedia events only come into existence through one's observation. In the electronic world we are merely internal observers, the world becomes an interface problem. The art product is not a picture anymore, it is not a two-dimensional window on the world but a door to multi-sensorial events; an artificial environment consisting of a dynamic system of different variables. One enters into a new kind of event horizon. These events can be visual, tactile, or audio. The observer is both an external and an internal observer — inside the event, part of the system that is observed.[4]

The problem, I fear, is that to make this (no doubt real) subjectivity apparent, we move from observing the work itself in all its intricacy and specificity to observing the epiphenomenon surrounding the work that is inherently more theoretical, abstract, and general. And, at least for me, the more we lose the visceral presence of an object and replace it with a more abstract concept, the less I feel drawn into an aesthetic vision, the less I feel that illusory empathic connection that draws me toward works of art.

Let's return to the other potential use of technology; we can think of this as the facilitative potential of technology. Even if we decide that great art might not be a likely product of new technologies that allow the roles of art-creator and art-perceiver to be merged, might technology make a meaningful difference in more traditional modes of art creation and consumption?

Without question, in the arts, as in all other branches of contemporary life, technology is everywhere. In some cases even relatively early advances made an enormous difference. It seems unnecessary to spell out how profoundly recordings have changed music, but what might be less evident is the effect of photocopying. In the bad old days, to make a score that could be reproduced easily, we had to use India ink on vellums (nonaffectionately known as onion skins). In order to "erase" mistakes, you had to wait for the ink to dry and then scratch it off with a razor blade. The ink pens were called Rapidographs (there were other brands as well, I suppose, but these were what I learned on), and they would leave a big dot of ink that would then smudge if you didn't blot the pen before almost every stroke. I can still see my entire hand and forearm covered with little black dots of ink. What made all of this worse was that when one made a significant mistake, it could mean redoing entire pages. Moreover, reproduction processes were expensive and of low quality. To get better printing you needed to make larger quantities than those needed for scores and parts that are mostly rented from the publishers. Only the most widely performed works could justify the huge cost of engraving. The advent of high-quality photocopying, which allowed pencil scores, transformed music publishing, as did computer engraving (using programs like Finale) a few years later. By now, I doubt that there is a single music publisher who has not switched to computer engraving of new scores.

The kind of change produced by computer engraving or photocopiers, however, will not make any fundamental difference in the situation for contemporary composers. It may make their life a little easier, or allow their publishers to achieve a financial equilibrium, but the basic situation we've been discussing throughout this volume is not meaningfully altered by these technologies.

Computer music[5] is another domain that you might expect me to mention, but, again, I do not think that this development changes the underlying sociological realities of making new music. Wonderful research centers for electronic or computer music have been created in universities and independently. They have allowed some amazing pieces of music to be created that possess sounds and effects undreamed of in earlier generations, but they still demand the kind of infrastructure and subsidies that other new music demands. In some ways, they make the situation even worse by enlarging the already great skill set a composer needs to acquire.

Some new technologies, though, might make a real difference to both the production and distribution of new art. While I suspect that the developments I am going to discuss in music have parallels in the other arts, I'll confine myself to music because I'm not really the person to present new technological developments in the other arts properly.

First, let's look at the production end. Classical music is not very expensive to write (even the most famous composer's commission fees are relatively modest), as long as we don't expect composers to live off the commissions and royalties they receive for their music. It is outrageously expensive to rehearse and perform, however. The amount of infrastructure used to create scores and parts, rehearse pieces, rent concert halls and percussion instruments (because percussionists play such a variety of instruments, they don't usually own them all, and so they are rented for concerts), tune pianos, make recordings, and so on, is enormous. I have spent a lot of time organizing concerts, and while the best of them are amazing experiences, a certain suspension of disbelief is required to justify such an expense for something that exists so briefly. This is a real disadvantage the performing arts have relative to the plastic arts.

One result of this situation is that composers have begun placing an ever-larger emphasis on recordings. Making recordings is usually at least as expensive as playing the pieces in concert, but the product is more durable. Certainly, recordings have greatly affected musical composition. Composers can become important figures even without being very widely performed. Many of the leading composers of our time gained their reputations at least as much through recordings as through concerts. I am dubious that acoustic music can achieve its full force in recordings, however, especially because the quality of home stereos has been relentlessly degraded as people buy ever-smaller equipment. What recordings do indisputably accomplish is to allow music from much farther afield to be vetted and compared in a classroom or when making programming decisions. Recordings have allowed composers to participate in a world market of music. We'll return to this when I talk about distribution, which is the greatest change to date in the music world.

Recording technology may help optimize the impact of the money being spent but won't change the basic financial equation (unless recordings manage to greatly enlarge the audience) that requires society to subsidize this kind of art for it to survive. What would change things is eliminating the performers. This is to a large extent what is happening on TV and movie soundtracks. Between sampling, synthesizers, and sequencers, it is possible for one person to realize a wide range of music without touching an acoustic instrument, and without even going into the whole world of new sounds that can be created through synthesis. Even when writing for solo piano, many composition students ask the computer to play them a model of the piece rather than going to the keyboard themselves.

This may not sound like such a bad idea (at least they are hearing their work) until you actually hear the results of these simulations. The problem is that learning to write for instruments is very much about learning the translation between the linear music notation system and the very nonlinear system that musicians and instruments propose. For a computer, playing two adjacent notes is no easier or harder than jumping from one end of the keyboard to the other. An impossibly quiet sound at the top of the flute's range is no harder for the computer to produce then a powerfully loud one at the bottom of its range. Moreover, the weight of notes is completely lost: Will it speak quickly or resist? Will a rhythm dissolve into texture or remain articulate? The homogenized sounds of even the best synthesizers give only very gross approximations of these attributes and no sense at all of the physicality or even possibility of the music. I have had students complain that the real performers don't play something as "well" as the simulation. These models are often a real barrier to the learning of instrumental writing (especially when students are not able to interact regularly with performers). A sculptor may well be able to make a wonderful model in clay of a sculpture that will ultimately be 60 feet high, but that doesn't mean the sculpture will be structurally sound once it is finally produced. That requires real knowledge of the materials that will be used in the final realization. If one imagines a computer-generated recording as the final product, however, most of those objections might sound old-fashioned.

One thing that would be indisputably lost if performers were minimized or eliminated from the composition-performance-recording process is the interaction between the work and interpretations of the work. One of the great virtues of the performing arts is that the work does not exist as a fixed object: rather it is perpetually recreated. Recordings have already blurred this aspect of music, but in the world of computer-generated sounds, the recording of a computer realization of a work (or even a composer performance of the work) may be the composer's only opportunity to hear it. While this might be a boon to those who have trouble getting their music played, composers, by eliminating the need for instrumentalists, would lose the much-needed direct contact with performers. Composers cannot master every instrument, they cannot be objective about decisions they have agonized over for months, and they cannot step outside themselves. Yet by interacting with performers, all these things are possible. An additional problem, if we get rid of the work for vast numbers of performers, is that we would then lose the justification for the whole system of musical training that is as essential to composers as well as performers. Although I love having the ability to integrate computer-generated sounds into instrumental works and additionally use computers to help work out nearly all of my music (though not through realistic simulations), I require some amount of interactivity with both the audience as well as the performers.

I fear the day when composers will stay behind their computer screens — isolated in their studios — from a piece's genesis all the way through to its realization. The tension that exists between composer's pushing and an audience's pulling may well be lost, and what now smacks of elitism may well degenerate into complete solipsism. A number of very successful compositions for tape alone have already been made, and while these works now represent a highly distinct genre, this is likely to change. If the concert experience were to become a rarity as high-speed Internet, wide-screen televisions, and home cinema systems proliferate, the line between static tape work and piece for performance would surely continue to blur. You may dismiss this possibility as akin to the current use of digital actors in films: a curiosity without much depth. It is likely, however, that the use of technology in musical composition will increase in the future as indicated by the increasing number of simulations of orchestra pieces submitted by applicants to graduate school. The real doubt is only how soon and how pervasively this trend will affect the musical world.

In one area, however, I think technology has already begun to make a meaningful and positive change for art: distribution. One of the reasons that really cutting-edge art has been limited to the world capitals is that those are the only places where you can find enough people to create a community of composers, performers, and listeners. The Internet has really changed this, however. I remember when I was in high school: A trip to New York or Chicago meant the possibility of going to a *real* record shop that would have a wide selection of contemporary music. Records, then CDs, would eat up nearly my whole budget on these trips. Now, of course, those stores are gone or don't carry much of a stock anymore. You can get just about anything that is available online, however. In one way this is a huge advantage, because even in its heyday Tower Records could not stock everything and all possible imports. But, of course, without the stores, you also lose the highly knowledgeable people who worked in them. With electronically connected individuals, however, one can still find virtual communities from whom advice can be solicited.

Moreover, the virtual community phenomenon is not confined to recordings. The rise of online communities means that a few thousand people scattered throughout the world can actually be reached in a coherent way: Look at how international festival audiences have become. If contemporary art music is doomed to speak to a shrinking audience, that audience is at least becoming more accessible. Even fifteen years ago you had to go to Paris if you wanted to know what was happening there; now it is nice to be there, but you can stay informed from almost anywhere.

A further advantage to this larger community is that it has raised the standards for composers. It is ever more difficult to stay a big fish in a small pond when the ponds keep linking up. Composers are more and more drawn into a world market. This is especially valuable in that it diminishes the role of personal ties (because you can't be friends with everyone, everywhere). For your music to succeed not just in one or two places but in many very different areas, it will have to be judged valuable by many different groups of listeners/critics/performers.

I doubt that better distribution will ever be able to make up for a society that does not have an interest in difficult art, but it can certainly help delay the worst effects of that attitude. Additionally, if things begin to change for the better, the effects could spread quite quickly. As much of the traditional publisher/record company infrastructure pulls out of this nongrowth business (the stock market is not content for a business to be viable; it must grow ever bigger), we at least can construct a jerry-rigged replacement that is cheaper and more flexible.

To conclude, I think technology will certainly have an impact on what artists do and how audiences learn about it and perhaps even experience it, but this will not be a sufficient change to alter the issues discussed earlier in this book. No matter how we learn about, receive, or interact with it, we still must be convinced that art can have great value and that the value has meaning beyond our preferences. Otherwise, we will simply increase the efficiency with which an overproduced, undesired commodity is marketed and distributed.

6

DESIGN SPACE

It has been drolly observed that linguists are unable to provide a convincing description of the grammar of language, yet young children can quickly master it. It also seems true that performers and listeners can understand music even though musicologists cannot agree what music means. The drollery is perhaps misplaced since there are many examples in physics, biology, and psychology of self-organizing systems which can converge on stable solutions to problems that defy formal analysis. Thus it should not be surprising that we do not yet understand the basis of many human skills. The history of ideas has shown that failures of understanding often arose from a poor initial perspective ...

— **L. Henry Shaffer**[1]

I've emphasized the idea of absolute aesthetic value and suggested that this might be a useful notion even if it is not "true" in some deep sense, but now I'd like to look a little bit at its potential reality and the constraints it might pose on art. I will move away from a more general discussion of artistic principles here and take most of my examples and ideas from music and from other fields only as they relate to music.

First, I should say that the existence of absolute criteria of worth does not mean that one true musical language or idiom exists, as some have tried to argue (notably Leonard Bernstein in his Norton Lectures at Harvard). At most it means that there may be general cognitive tools and principles that, when combined with auditory perception, place constraints on what is perceivable and thus potentially meaningful. Furthermore, this might offer a sense in which value-laden words like "richness," "complexity," "formal-coherence," even perhaps "beauty," might have a real, almost universal meaning — at least until we meet some extraterrestrials.

How could this be? If we want to speak about anything absolute, we need to postulate a sort of unitary framework that is deeper than the apparently very diverse surfaces of different musical idioms. Only if we find some sorts of perceptual and/or cognitive universals, or at least quasi-universals, can we hope to find any sort of absolute criteria that could be the source of aesthetic value. We need to imagine some universal musical language toolkit that allows the construction of a vast, if not infinite, number of different languages. Is such a thing plausible or even possible? In this chapter, I propose to look at some of the reasons why I believe it is and some of the tools we might possess. Moreover, I will begin to move our discussion from why listeners should support music that is something other than pure entertainment to how composers might go about creating art that tries to merit this support.

Let me say right off the bat that the word "language," which I will use liberally, presents an imperfect analogy at best. In language one finds a clear duality between the mechanisms of communication (grammar) and the content being communicated. With music, this division, though perhaps present, is anything but clear. It may still be worthwhile, however, to think about music for a moment as if it were a language. We can think of a particular musical idiom as having forms, harmonies, idiomatic musical expressions, and gestures that confirm or contradict learned expectations, all of which can be related to parallel linguistic and literary structures. Furthermore, it is at least plausible that in the same way that human linguistic symbol manipulation machinery can be customized for English, French, or Navajo, our musical machinery can be trained in classical music, Balinese gamelan, or hip-hop.

In the domain of language, Noam Chomsky famously said that from a Martian perspective all humans speak one language. The linguist Steve Pinker describes what Chomsky means in this way:

> Chomsky's claim that from a Martian's-eye-view all humans speak a single language is based on the discovery that the same symbol manipulating machinery, without exception, underlies the world's languages. Linguists have long known that the basic design features of language are found everywhere. [...] Languages use the mouth-to-ear channel as long as the users have intact hearing (manual and facial gestures, of course, are the substitute channel used by the deaf). A common grammatical code, neutral between production and comprehension, allows speakers to produce any linguistic message they can understand, and vice versa. Words have stable meanings, linked to them by arbitrary convention. Speech sounds are treated discontinuously; a sound that is acoustically halfway between *bat* and *pat* does not mean something halfway between batting and patting. Languages can convey meanings that are abstract and remote in time or space from the speaker. Linguistic forms are infinite in number, because they are created by a discrete combinatorial system. Languages all show a duality of patterning in which one rule system is used to order phonemes within morphemes, independent of meaning, and another is used to order morphemes within words and phrases, specifying their meaning.[2]

Pinker then goes far beyond these design features to include other common attributes across all human languages: large vocabularies, parts of speech including nouns and verbs, phrases organized according to something called the X-bar system (which we don't need to go into here) as well as "the higher levels of phrase structure including auxiliaries, which signify tense, modality, aspect and negation. [...] New word structures can be created and modified by derivational and inflectional rules. [...] The phonological forms of words are defined by metrical and syllable trees [...] their details [...] found in language after language [...], give a strong impression that a Universal Grammar [...] underlies the human language instinct."[3]

Pinker specifically wants to put language in a very different category than music, which he thinks of as an "artificial system" like a computer language. However, here, I believe, he is wrong. Much to the chagrin of some composers, music does not work simply through an arbitrary set of logical rules like a computer language. Some musical systems seem "learnable," while others seem like just the sort of artificial construct Pinker calls all music. So although musical language is indeed very different from human language, I believe that there are real parallels.

To highlight the convergence between the human language instinct and the human musical instinct, we need to look at what "basic design features" might underlie the world's musical languages. Basic design features are not quite the same as the often-discussed universals; they are more like potential universals, or elements contained in a universal toolkit. Polyphony is a good example: Humans clearly seem capable of processing multiple simultaneous melodic lines when those lines are at least somewhat related harmonically and not too large in number. And while many types of music take advantage of this capability (choral hymns, Bach fugues, jazz combos, etc.), many others do not (Gregorian chants, college fight-songs, "house" music, etc.).

One feature present in most music is pitch. If I say to you that pitch is an important musical feature, you will probably be tempted to say, "So what?" You probably think of pitch as such an obvious part of the sounds in the world that we would necessarily use it in our music. The traditional view of music often treats pitch as if it were a sort of unitary atom possessed by and characterizing all sounds: as if a sound and a pitch were essentially the same thing. In fact, we tend to think of the pitch description of a note or sound as somehow being, if not complete, at least sufficient to describe the note or sound. This is why many musical notation systems show little else. Most sounds in the world, however, fall more into the category of noise than pitch. In order for a sound to produce the sensation of pitch, its sonic constituents must approximate a particular "harmonic" relationship (integer multiples of a fundamental frequency). A sound with energy distributed less regularly in terms of frequency will be nonpitched like the wind, a door slamming, breaking glass, breathing, purring, a cymbal crash, a bass drum "hit," and so on. A violin or flute is very good at producing pitch (although even with these instruments the nonpitched part of the sound — bow or breath noise — is still significant), but this is because we designed and built these instruments with just that purpose in mind. You might also think we focus on pitch because of the human voice, but only vowel sounds contain clear pitch and a great deal of our vocalizations including all consonants are very noisy.

From a perspective parallel to language, we can see that pitch is a very useful thing for music to employ. Because of the specificity of relation between the internal components of a pitched sound, it is much easier to separate two pitches into distinct sources than it is to separate noise sounds. When our ears receive a complex sound signal from out in the world, they can more easily divide up the auditory "scene" into its various constituent elements (a clarinet note, a violin note, a piano note, etc.) if the internal logic of each of those notes is simple, as it is with a pitched note. This separation of the auditory stream that reaches our ear into distinct sonic objects is at the heart of how our auditory system analyzes the world. We have no trouble hearing the TV droning in the background while still following a conversation, and realizing the dog is barking because he wants to be taken for a walk. Our ears and minds have multiple and overlapping strategies for performing this task, which psychologists call auditory stream segregation. But in a situation where all the sounds are coming from approximately the same distance and direction (say, from an ensemble on a concert stage), the internal coherence of a structure like pitch is a huge help. You can test this for yourself; just try asking two or three friends to stand across the room and sing different notes. See if you can hear who is singing what. Now ask them to blow unpitched air, making a windlike noise, and try to sort out who is making what sound. You may well succeed, but it will be much harder, and if you multiplied the number of "sources," this processing advantage would become very significant.

If you want to go beyond the first level of sensory perception and build a more layered cognitive structure, notes can be treated discontinuously (categorically) like speech sounds, which presents a huge advantage. When a jazz singer sings his or her "out-of-tune" blue note, we do not hear a different pitch from the one specified by the scale, and we also do not hear a hybrid between two members of the scale on either side of the "blue note": We hear the expected pitch with an inflection that carries expressive meaning. This is a very close parallel to what happens in language, where, as Pinker said, "A sound that is acoustically halfway between *bat* and *pat* does not mean something halfway between batting and patting." This is why, although we could understand the speech of almost any speaker, some, like James Earl Jones, get paid large sums of money to read for television commercials, because their voices seem to communicate more than just the discrete linguistic content.

Pitched notes organized into a limited number of categories have other advantages as well. Many musical cultures generalize notes across register through a principle called octave equivalency. This is the principle that lets us think of middle C on a piano as being in a sense the "same" note as a high C on a piccolo. With octave equivalency, men with low voices and women with high voices can sing the "same" tune in the "same" key but in different registers. Neuroscientist Jamshed Bharucha has even used his self-organizing neural net model to show that octave equivalency can form just through untutored exposure to the acoustical structure of pitched notes without any conceptual or theoretical predisposition. Perhaps more significantly, pitches and octave equivalency allow us to divide the frequency spectrum into a small number of related notes. Different cultures do this in different ways and some don't do it at all, but the vast majority of music in the world is organized according to these hierarchical arrangements of pitches called scales. When scales are deployed in music, they can create the hierarchical sensation of key.

Music that uses a scale to produce a sense of key usually shares some additional design features. The scales tend to have between five and seven distinct scale member pitches. This should not be surprising, since five to seven seems to be just the right number of units for human working memory (think of phone numbers or zip codes, or the common representation of dates, etc.).[4] There are some entities we tend to call scales that don't have this "magic" number of notes, like the twelve-note chromatic scale (all the notes in one octave on the piano). However, the chromatic scale is not really a scale in that it cannot generate a key: All the notes in it are equivalent. By this I mean that whatever note you begin or end on, the chromatic scale always contains exactly the same pitches and relationships, so one never has a sense of one note being more important, more tense, more final, and so on, than another. This same problem exists for the whole-tone scale and several other so-called symmetrical scales like the octatonic scale: In all of these scales, the collection of notes does not allow a unique set of relations between each scale member and the other scale-degrees. Thus, it should not be a surprise that when you look at how these "scales" are used in pieces of music it is never to generate a key. These symmetrical scales seem to be used for ornamentation and color, while a more limited or specific collection of pitches creates the sense of key.

Sandra Trehub and others did a series of studies exploring why this might be the case and found that infants can detect mistuned notes much better within even completely unfamiliar scales made up of unequal steps than within equal-step scales. Adults are better with the familiar unequal-step scales like the major and minor scales, but equally bad at all unfamiliar scales. They interpret this result as showing an inherent processing bias towards unequal-step scales that allows the learning of particular unequal-step scales as we grow older.[5] It is certainly tempting to see this as something like what happens with linguistic phonemes. There seems to be a limited repertoire of potential human phonemes, which is nonetheless much larger than the set used by any given language. Although all human babies are born with the capacity to learn any of these phonemes, there seems to be a critical period beginning at around nine months of age and stretching until around age two when babies start to permanently lose the ability to hear any and every possible human phoneme. They start to focus exclusively on the subset of phonemes used in the languages they have been hearing spoken by those around them and which they will soon begin to speak. Within a very short time they even lose the ability to differentiate some phonemes that they could have easily differentiated a few weeks earlier. They have pared down a large space of potential language sounds into a smaller but deeper set of usable and understandable ones. By limiting the number of meaningful categories, we allow inflection of those categories both for the sake of meaning (the verbal equivalent of the musical "blue-note" already mentioned) and robustness (the equivalent of my being able to recognize the tune based on its general contour in spite of my mother's out-of-tune humming).

Keylike hierarchical systems often have the added virtue of allowing us to attribute sensations like tension or incompleteness to various scale degrees. While these properties, at least for tonal music, are probably learned in a harmonic context, the association causes us to feel functional associations when we hear even unaccompanied single-line melodies. The psychologist Carol Krumhansl has done a lot of work in mapping out these relations into multidimensional "pitch-spaces."[6] Jamshed Bharucha has used self-organizing neural nets to show that this can plausibly happen without any prompting from a music theory teacher. The nets learn to recognize scale degrees and even to follow modulations like we do. They were able (just through self-organization) to go beyond individual notes to recognize the scale-degree function of chords. In fact, Bharucha also showed that a set of hierarchical associations and expectations analogous to that of tonality is formed by these neural nets when they are trained with Indian ragas instead of Western tonal melodies.[7] These learned key systems with their accompanying sensations are clearly very important to our perception of music, but I suspect the more basic design feature that allows the mind to form these networks is tension.

Tension is clearly very important to many types of music, but it can be hard to speak about from a common vantage point. When you take a traditional harmony class, tension is almost always taught in a grammatical way: This chord requires that resolution, that one is incomplete without this, like linked clauses in a sentence. Tension can be generated in all sorts of ways in all different art forms (contextual tension, physical tension, emotional tension, etc.), but here I want to confine myself to harmonic tension in music. In the mid-1990s, I was collaborating with an American expat psychologist then based in France, Steve McAdams, on some studies looking at harmonic tension in unfamiliar music. He and his students ran some pilot studies to try to determine how they should explain tension to the experimental subjects who were going to rate the relative tension of chord pairs. What he found was that if he tried to call listeners' attention to any of the specific features that might contribute to tension, they came to very different conclusions about the relative tension of chords. When he just said "tension" and told them to define it in their own way, however, they agreed almost perfectly on how relatively tense the chords were. This leads me to believe that in mental terms some underlying reality to this category exists even if we cannot easily create a direct mapping onto one particular set of sonic features.

Harmonic tension, like pitch, almost certainly begins with a perceptual phenomenon — in this case roughness. Roughness is produced by simultaneously sounding components of the total sound-field that fall close together within what is called the critical band. Because of the way the ear works, these neighboring sounds interfere with each other and produce a parasitic amplitude modulation called "beating." Piano tuners count the beats-per-second between notes to tune a piano in equal temperament. (If you listen to the beating between the C below middle C and the E above it, it should beat 5.5 times per second — I was taught to think of this as the speed of saying "Denver-to-Milwaukee" moderately quickly.) Roughness is something many other animals also are sensitive to, including cats and starlings.

If you look at the roughness produced by intervals played on a piano, you will see that the total amount of roughness corresponds very closely with the perceived dissonance of each interval. What is surprising, though, is that if you play these same intervals with very pure sounds made by sine-tone generators lacking all sonic richness (upper partials for the more technically minded) that caused the roughness in the first place, musically trained listeners will make the same dissonance judgments as they did with more realistic complex sounds, while inexperienced listeners will not. Inexperienced listeners will tend to judge any sounds that lie entirely outside of the critical band as consonant even if these same sounds played by real instruments with rich timbres would have produced roughness, because some of the sonic components (rich sounds are complex and consist of many internal components) would fall within the critical band. This is true even for intervals we usually categorize as very dissonant, like the major seventh.

This seems to suggest that we can all perceive roughness and learn to associate that roughness with musical structures, even if the roughness is later removed. None of this should be too surprising to anyone who has ever watched a black-and-white TV: Although color is clearly

a part of how we perceive the difference between the animate skin of a
person's face and the cold gray of stone, we have no trouble seeing the
gray face of the TV program as full of life because we have already seen
so many Technicolor faces and have other cues for knowing that it is a
human face.

Western tonal music offers a familiar example of this. If you are
in C-major, a G-major triad will sound tense, even though acoustically it is no different from the relaxed C-major triad. The reason is
almost certainly that the triad built on the fifth scale degree is often
accompanied by a seventh scale degree that introduces extra roughness.
Because we have heard the dominant seventh chord (the version with
that extra, dissonant note) so often in this context, the perception of
tension remains even without the psychophysical cause.

For those of you who have never really studied music, this may seem
to be incredible, but you can experience these degrees of tension very
easily yourself. Take almost any recording of a classical piece and play
the final section until the second-to-last chord (it may be easier to start
at the beginning of the next piece and scan backwards to get to the last
thirty seconds or so of the piece). If you play the recording until this
second-to-last chord, but stop it before the final chord, it will likely
sound very unfinished. This is due to a particular use of the tension I've
been describing. If you now play the end of the piece again, you should
be able to feel your gut unclenching ever so slightly as the tension of
the penultimate chord gives way to the release of the final chord. You
will have something like this experience with almost any tonal piece,
even though the particular identities of the more tense chords and the
less tense chords will be different and sometimes interchanged.

You will no doubt have seen the pattern I'm suggesting by now: A physical or perceptual reality creates a bias toward the adoption of certain types
of cognitive structures for use in the development of musical language.

Approximate rhythmic regularity, quasi-periodicity if you will, is
another very common feature of music, and one might argue that it
comes about in this same way. (Traditional theory refers to this as
"pulse" and usually treats it more as an assumed axiom than a motivated choice; we mainly refer to the pulse on those occasions when
the composer chooses to mask or contradict the prevailing pulsation.)

While I would imagine that heartbeats, breathing, and other quasi-periodic phenomena that are part of our daily life may lie at the origin of our attention to regular rhythm, I think that the reason we use them in so many different musical traditions has to do more with a processing advantage similar to the one bestowed by asymmetric scales of pitch. We're not very good at making rhythmic judgments about the length of two notes in a vacuum. Ask someone to take a stopwatch and sing one note for 6 seconds and another for 6.5 seconds. Tell them to mix up the order and try to guess which one is which without tapping your foot or counting smaller units: Just try to hear which note sounds longer. I'd bet that if you really refrain from counting, you'll hear the second note as longer whether it was or not. Now have them tap seconds with their hand while singing the two notes, and you'll see that there is not the slightest difficulty in distinguishing the two durations; in fact, you could easily tell 6 seconds and 6.05 seconds apart with a reliable metronome, because one would end right on the beat and the other would end just after the beat. Rhythm, like 5 to 7 note asymmetric scales, is also an aid for our processing of musically useful information — in this case, in the time domain.

In many musical systems, we add further levels of related hierarchy. In the pitch domain, multiple keys can be organized hierarchically into a sort of larger metaset of relations called a pitch-space. Pulses are almost always organized into groups of two, three, or four in what we call a metrical grid. In each case we have taken the power of the local relation and given it a higher-level function. While this is certainly very different from language, it shows the same sort of uniform toolkit. In fact, because music does not possess the direct information coding of language, the universal-musical-tools exhibit effects at larger time-scales and higher levels of structure, like musical form. Think of how many types of music take advantage of contrasts between fast and slow, tense and relaxed, lyrical and rhythmic. Also note that while the pulse speeds of music vary quite a bit, it is not by a factor of 100, or even 20. The slowest pieces will tend to have a pulse of 20 to 30 beats per minute and anything faster than 240 beats per minute is very rare. Moreover, slower pieces tend to have more subdivisions per beat, making the difference in average note density even less. Again one suspects that the natural motor ability of performers has much to do with this constraint, but regardless of the origin it has become part of the language.

This is not the place to seek comprehensiveness in mapping out the basic design features of musical language; I have just been trying to convince you that some such set of principles does exist. My motivation is that if such principles exist in any absolute sense, the way in which a particular musical language uses them might affect its possibilities of being meaningful, and the way a particular work interacts with the underlying mental principles might be capable of making it successful or not in some absolute way. Now you will notice that just like linguists, I am forced into post hoc reasoning in trying to determine these design principles. No musician (at least prior to recent ones) set out to deconstruct the underlying principles of music in order to write it; instead, they could depend on an enormous body of empirical data generated by the musical tradition to which they belonged. In fact, in the twentieth century advocates of a return to tonality were often forceful in arguing that new musical languages were simply not "understandable." (In this context "understandable" might be read as "coherent.") They maintained that much contemporary music has given up the very elements that lead to a listener having a "musical experience." While it is tempting to dismiss these arguments as reactionary, self-serving, or narrow-minded, they have greatly influenced the discourse of most composers and music theorists. (For those with more of a music theory background, I would suggest that from a certain perspective, one might view much of PC set theory as an attempt to "prove" the coherent and structured nature of the atonal and twelve-tone repertory.[8]) Rather than dismiss or attempt to "disprove" this argument, however, it might be better to admit that there may be an element of truth that, if properly evaluated and understood, might impact in a positive way the development of musical languages not derived from the tonal model.

The perspective I have adopted in speaking about a universal design-toolkit for music is borrowed from evolutionary psychology and evolutionary theory. Perhaps an even better analogy for how these basic principles interact with potential musical languages comes straight from evolutionary theory. Richard Dawkins in his book *The Blind Watchmaker* talks about the metaphor of design space. By this

he means the theoretical multidimensional space in which each potential characteristic that an organism could develop is represented on a
separate dimension. And while any *possible* organism would be situ-
ated somewhere within this space, it is not a limitless space, where any
attribute or combination of attributes is possible — where cows can
sprout a spacesuit and fly over the moon. Evolutionary design space
is constrained by embryology, past events, current conditions, and a
plethora of other things that guarantee that the vast number of possible
designs is not the unbounded, unstructured chaos of Borges's "Library
of Babel." Some creatures that are easily imaginable, like dragons, do
not seem to be accessible to evolution. (DNA would have a tough time
specifying an asbestos-lined throat.) In our musical analogy, we might
be able to create almost any sound, at least with a computer, but these
sounds are not necessarily capable of functioning — in the sense of creating a musical sensation in a listener.

In all fields of applied design (and music is in a sense the applied
design of sound), "design space" can be used to designate the range of
solutions that satisfy the design criteria. The dimensions are not fully
independent or even necessarily continuous: If you make SUVs taller
so the people driving them can feel powerful and safe, you will almost
inevitably raise the center of gravity and make it easier for the trucks
to flip over in an accident — thus reducing the driver's actual safety.
Design features that may seem very different can be linked at these
deeper levels, and it may not be possible to treat them independently.
There may well be no region of the design space with a tall car and a low
center of gravity. An understanding of this space can help us see how
almost inevitable certain design solutions are (the philosopher Daniel Dennett calls them "forced moves in design space") and may let us
appreciate how special and unique other regions of the space might be.

Evolutionary theorists use this concept when trying to disentangle
two similar creatures whose resemblance might be caused by converging lines of development within a small design space or might be the
result of related development within a potentially large design space.
Put another way, when two creatures resemble each other in some
respect, it might be because they are closely related or it might be
because they are both trying to accomplish some similar task that can

only be done in a few ways. Streamlining is one of the classical examples given to illustrate a small design space. Fish, whales, birds, cars (at least since the advent of computer modeling and wind tunnels), and airplanes all seem to share a related set of smoothly curved shapes called "streamlined." This resemblance is due not to tradition, imitation, or shared lineage, but is the result of an attempt to accomplish the same goal — reducing drag on motion through a viscous medium, water or air — and streamlining is an effective means to that end, perhaps the most effective means. This distinction between the two possible explanations for similarity (relation or forced moves) is very important for us, because relational similarity tells us only about history, while the forced moves help us map out the boundaries of design space.

What is important from my point of view as a composer is that this may be a way of understanding the constraints, if any, on comprehensible musical compositions. In other words, what are the limits to the design space in which coherent musical languages may be created? Or, how can we create these languages while avoiding the Scylla and Charybdis of renouncing the potential for innovation versus creating impossible artificial grammars that can be studied but never "learned." If music that has absolute aesthetic value really exists, are there constraints on it or could it be anything that someone can imagine? I am, of course, not posing this question in a vacuum. A whole series of musical styles from the twentieth century takes starting points in combinatorial mathematics or chance-related procedures, or a host of other extramusical sources. Some critics have attacked exemplars of these musical styles as "unhearable." Rather than debating the "validity" of specific styles, the more interesting question is the general one: If we admit that some sequences of notes that may be logically coherent are not musically coherent even in principle, is it possible to determine the "design space" in which a musical language must reside to be viable? Furthermore, is it possible to use this information to design a musical language that is both novel and comprehensible?

We ought to start with what we know. At least one elaborately developed musical language exists that most listeners agree is learnable and capable of producing satisfying musical results: tonality. While it goes far beyond the scope of this book to address the common-practice heritage in detail, a few observations are necessary. Tonal music — like most other music in the world — was created through a long process of trial and error, in which the successful efforts of the current generation were assimilated both by contemporary and succeeding generations: It was not created by an individual who "dreamed it up" and expected the world to learn it and adapt to it. In spite of stylistic differences between composers like Mozart and Beethoven, enough similarity between the various composers of a given generation and even across generations existed to allow one composer's insights to be profitably applied to another's dilemma and to allow one composer's failures to forestall another composer's attempt. Ideas that failed to function for performers and/or audiences had little chance of enduring. This golden era of collaborative research and development (of course the participants in this R&D would certainly not have seen it in this way) created a vast base of knowledge about what types of musical ideas, structures, and materials could be employed in effective musical works. Though it was only later and gradually that this knowledge became codified in theoretical terms, the pedagogical practices that depended on study of older works and style imitation leave little doubt that most of what a composer did was based on what others had done. This knowledge was both liberating and constraining.

Composers were free to create novel structures of vast proportions without incurring a correspondingly greater degree of risk — because while the overall design might be novel, the elements were all well tested. Risk may be a difficult notion to assess relative to a musical work, but it is nonetheless real. Without the experience of other composers, one would have little hope of creating forms that could hold a listener's attention over time, create large-scale relations, impart a sense of departure and return, and so on. At least from the perspective of a tonal composer, the lack of any of these elements would have constituted a serious failure. Just as structural principles of construction do not hinder an architect from building a novel geometry on a traditionally designed foundation, composers in the later part of the nineteenth century were not impeded from pushing the organizing principles of tonality far from their roots while still profiting from the structural principles that allow tension to be maintained over long time-scales.

However, in the twentieth century many composers began to lose sight of the reasons that had motivated the choices made by tonal composers. The materials of tonal composition that had been superbly designed for compelling reasons (at the time) became blind articles of faith separated from their raison d'être for many twentieth-century composers. In recent years, although a few composers have continued to ignore the contradiction created by preserving the symptom without the cause (making a virtual religion out of the permutation of an inherited set of symbolic elements drawn from traditional Western notation), many have tried to address the issue.[9] The rise of neoromanticism, postmodernism, and other movements that return to tonal principles reflects an awareness of this problem. The composers belonging to these movements have recognized the futility of using the tonal model to write a music that shares few, if any, common goals with the music for which that model was developed. Their solution has been to restore the foundation and return to tried-and-true methods of musical construction.

George Rochberg expressed this concern to me. Like many listeners, he said that he remembered a lot of music of Brahms or Beethoven, but that so much new music just faded away after he heard it, leaving nothing. He felt that an effective model should create music that sticks to you like burrs to your clothing after a walk in the woods. He saw no reason to build on what he saw as failed modernism, when successful older styles remained viable.

Other composers have confronted this same problem — which of the inherited materials of tonality still make sense in the context of their music and which should be jettisoned and replaced with novel devices — through highly personal and sometimes eccentric means. Composers like Conlon Nancarrow, Harry Partch, or Iannis Xenakis opted for a difficult and lonely course, turning away from our inherited tools to prospect in solitude for usable principles of compositional construction. These "mavericks" have sometimes produced remarkable results. The languages they developed, though, have turned out to be extremely personal, individual visions, and as such they have not formed the foundation of any broad movements to rival tonality, Indian classical music, or other systems. While this does not reduce the artistic impact of their oeuvre, it does limit the usefulness these composers offer as a model for other composers whose aims deviate even slightly from their own. This should not be surprising, because it seems very unlikely that these isolated figures can hope to build anything approaching the depth or scope of tonal music. Tonality was developed by thousands of composers over hundreds of years and has received millions of hours of field-testing with audiences. It would be hard for even the most brilliant intuitions to rival the strength and depth of that collective effort (and it is astounding that sometimes this has happened).

However, another solution may be suggested again through our analogy with the study of design space. Today's architects and structural engineers don't need to build endless models and perform impossible calculations; improved technology changed the givens. It is now possible to accurately model a complex and completely novel structure and yet still know if it will stand (think of any building by Frank Gehry). Theories are available that can give predictive and not simply descriptive information. If both abstract criteria and design constraints exist that create the background in which those criteria can be evaluated, it may be possible to create work that is both meaningful and novel: Look at the range of forms that suspension bridges can take, while all using the same set of principles.

If we want to understand the design space of musical language, we are going to have to reverse engineer some of the world's musical traditions. Any tradition that has endured over time must on some level "function" for its listeners. By studying the music, we ought to be able to deduce some of the principles that allow it to function. Our goal as composers ought not to be the goal of music theorists, who want to understand the language itself; composers need to discover the first principles that allow the language to function. We want to understand the "whys" rather than the "hows," so that we can create new ways of satisfying those same design criteria. This will not be sufficient information for us, however, because it is not just the language that will need to be developed, but also the content — and the two are intertwined in complex ways in a piece of music. Before we look at my personal deductions and the first principles that seem most important to me, we need to look at what the word "meaning" might mean in a musical context. In discussing comprehensible or learnable languages, we must remember that it is perfectly feasible to write an uninteresting novel with correct grammar. The linguistic framework cannot provide anything more than the point of departure for a compositional elaboration. Great music must do more than function: It has to inspire.

7

"UNDERSTANDING" MUSIC

What I like about music is its ability to be convincing, to carry an argument through successfully to the finish, though the terms of the argument remain unknown quantities.

—John Ashbery

Music, not being made up of objects nor referring to objects, is intangible and ineffable; it can only be, as it were, inhaled by the spirit: the rest is silence.

—Jacques Barzun

In Chapter 6, we discussed music as something like a language, but in order for that metaphor to be viable we need to discuss further what it might mean to "understand" a piece of music (or even a single musical idea). When I use a word and you listen to it, we will be objectively communicating only if we agree almost exactly on what the words mean. If we are to deal with the kind of subjective communication that takes place during a musical experience, we are going to need some help defining our terms. Although it often seems that philosophical concepts can obfuscate more than clarify, in this case they might help.

Philosophy has a word for subjective personal experiences: *qualia*, the subjective "quality" of an experience, what it feels like. There is also a word for coded communication like language: *semantic*, referring to categories and labels, not the subjective experience that elements bearing those labels evoke. It is very easy to explain semantically why the sunset produces colors (perhaps not for me, but certainly for any physicist who understands the light emitted by the sun and its interaction with the atmosphere). However, it is completely impossible to explain why it is beautiful or why watching it is pleasurable. This is not to say it cannot be discussed at all, just that a clear semantic explanation (the sunset is beautiful because the light at this frequency provokes, etc.) cannot be formulated for the qualia of a subjective percept. Even an evolutionary "just-so" story about why it might be advantageous to find the sunset beautiful, or a neuroscientific description of neuron activation patterns, would not really answer the qualitative question of why we find it beautiful. Every painting of a sunset is, in fact, a more or less successful attempt to communicate the qualia of beauty produced in the artist by that event.

A musical performance is a somewhat parallel attempt by the performer to communicate to the members of the audience the qualia he or she experiences when hearing a musical composition: It is the single most relevant and eloquent way to discuss the real "meaning" of a piece of music. While the added complexity of having the three layers of composer, performer, and audience complicates the relations to some degree, anyone who has studied an instrument will have had at least a hint of this experience of purely aesthetic communication. A typical lesson embodies a dynamic back-and-forth between student and teacher: The student plays; the teacher says "no, like this," then plays; the student tries to emulate the teacher's performance, or resists and goes a different way until an agreement or perhaps a surrender has been achieved. A real discussion has taken place and real information has been exchanged — even if we cannot put it into words.

Because I'm not there and we cannot hold this discussion around a piano or even a hi-fi, the first question we have to address is what, if anything, can we discuss semantically (our only option in this situation) about pieces of music that might be of value. So much of our thinking is semantic in nature — we think in words — that we should probably ask ourselves whether semantic knowledge impacts the subjective experience of listening to music at all and, if so, in what ways?

The answers to these questions are not direct. Semantic knowledge is clearly useful in that it can give referents. I can explain that a musical motive is called "x" and then refer to it without having to play it for you. Categorizing things this way will unquestionably aid memory (this is a form of the chunking that we discussed earlier). Semantic knowledge of a piece of music and its score will also help us separate the authorial voice from the interpretive voice. Moreover, it will help us think about the work's relationship to other pieces even when their surfaces are quite different — although one still might wonder if any of this allows us to listen "better."

What does it mean to listen well? Paying attention is certainly a big part of it. Letting music wash over you may be pleasant, but you will only perceive the tip of the iceberg. There are all kinds of things one can hear without any special knowledge or skill, and, ultimately, it is the sensation produced in each moment as you attentively listen that will matter.

I do not believe that charting out forms and labeling themes will help you very much in listening to and enjoying a piece of music — just as making an outline will not make you love a novel with a complicated plot. Decoding how the composer built the piece also will not guarantee a more satisfying experience. One might be tempted to listen for clues to the composer's life or emotional state; though this may be interesting, you probably will not love or hate a piece based on whether or not it was written while the composer played skittles. You love a work because of the sensations or qualia it produces when you hear it. Therefore, I believe you can get more out of close listening by starting with the affective, subjective experience the work creates in your mind. In a certain sense it will not even matter if the affects in the piece you love were intentional compositional choices or by-products of some other process or even just happy accidents.

If we go ahead and remove intentions, circumstance, as well as the detailed recipes for writing the music (*la cuisine*, in French) from our discussion of understanding a piece, it might seem we are taking away your best listening strategies. What is left to the close listener to listen for? The answer, I believe, comes from the way Daniel Dennett and others use the term "intensions" (with an *s*). We can't really know what a composer intends. If you believe the psychoanalysts, maybe the composer himself did not know what he intended. We *can*, however, know what affects the piece produces in us when we hear it. Moreover, we can imagine that creating this result (the affect) was the composer's intent. Therefore, rather than calling this projected intent a real *intention*, we will use the funny philosophical lingo and call it an *intension*.

If you listen to a composer's "intensions," you can look at a piece from the viewpoint of an industrial spy. Here is the finished piece that produced a specific affect in you, the listener, and the question is how. At this point we no longer care about the composer's intentions; we are assuming that the bit of music in question is a machine designed to produce an affect, and through reverse engineering we want to know how it was done. This so-called "intensional stance" removes the question of "why" without upsetting the supremacy of effect over cause. It is "as-if" the piece was designed to make these affects, because they are why we listen to it and care about it.

Even more traditional, semantic-oriented, analytical schemes will eventually need to address affect and the ways it is produced, but they are often hampered by a rigid framework that can force our judgments into a narrow mold. We tend to break our way of listening and analyzing into two opposing viewpoints. The two quotes at the start of this chapter represent the two ways that musical meaning has traditionally been discussed. These views are usually presented in oppositional terms, and the words used to describe them say a lot about on which side of the divide you situate yourself. Some of the ways this dichotomy is presented are:

German vs. French
Discursive vs. Decorative
Developmental vs. Static
Expressionist vs. Impressionist

In each case, though, the conceptual divide is basically the same. Do you appreciate the object itself on an aesthetic level, or do you use the object as a tool to comment or explicate some other thing or idea? Debussy advised that if you want to understand nature, you should watch a sunset, not listen to Beethoven's "Pastoral" Symphony, while I suspect that Adorno would have given the opposite advice. Which gives us another way of framing the divide: Does art help us understand the world or ourselves, or does it give us something that is wonderful but distinct from other aspects of the world — existing in some aesthetic realm? Is the object itself only the surface of a meaningful dialectical network of meaning, or is it the entire work? In this, as in all dialectical presentations, both sides, in fact, capture some of the truth.

This debate is a little like those representations of a 3-D cube (figure 7.1) that we all doodle (its official name is a Necker cube in honor of the nineteenth-century Swiss crystallographer who discovered the illusion): You can see it one way or the other way, but not both ways. You can flip your vision of a Necker cube back and forth, seeing the dot in either the left front corner or the left rear corner, but you cannot see it in both places at once. (Think of the lower square as being in the foreground and look, then think of the upper square as being in the foreground and look again.)

All this is still a bit abstract. Let's demonstrate this binary way of perceiving as it is applied to the analysis of musical forms. I'm going to talk in more specific ways about music than I have up until this point, but I will try to make sure it remains understandable. I'll mention some

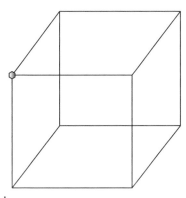

Figure 7.1 The Necker cube.

musical examples, but they will be taken from very famous works you can readily find at any music store, library, or on the Web. We will analyze a form in the traditional discursive manner, then discuss briefly a piece that calls for a different, less directional sort of analysis. After presenting this fairly standard way of using these different perspectives on repertoire to which they are well suited, we will discuss how the two views might in fact be more complementary than we tend to think — even for pieces normally considered as belonging to one or the other camp. Then we will look at how the manner in which we analyze or listen to a work may condition our expectations in ways that interfere with really hearing a piece on its own terms. Finally, I'll try to offer a less conditioning framework for attentive listening.

The most famous of all musical forms is the "sonata" form; anyone who has had any sort of music appreciation class or read much in the way of program notes has at least seen references to this form. This form earned the name because it is generally used in the first move-ment of instrumental sonatas (which are sets of movements for a solo instrument or an accompanied instrument that were very popular from the late eighteenth through the nineteenth centuries). Sonata form was probably the most important form in all types of large-scale instru-mental works throughout the classical and Romantic periods, so the name is something of a misnomer: Concertos and symphonies use sonata form as much as sonatas.

If we look at sonata form from the traditional viewpoint (which we could also call the German viewpoint) we have two ways of describ-ing it: harmonically or thematically (motivically). In either case, we will divide the movement into three parts: exposition-development-recapitulation. The exposition presents some material and is often immediately repeated in its entirety. It also serves to move the piece away from the key in which it started to another closely related har-monic region. The development takes tunes or tune-fragments from the exposition and transforms them in various ways that can be more or less clearly linked to the original form of these tunes (occasionally new themes are even introduced). The development will typically go through a number of different, less closely related key areas, but will not return to the original key. The recapitulation follows the development and presents a more or less precise repetition of the exposition (though often shortened). The recapitulation begins in the original key and, unlike the exposition, also ends in that key. While the exposition is repeated by itself (expo-expo), the development and recapitulation are often repeated together as a unit (dev-recap-dev-recap).

When analyzing a sonata form movement from a harmonic point of view, we focus on the notion of departure and return. We will still need to refer to thematic material, but we will be more concerned with the tonal space that material occupies than with the nature of the material itself. We might even look for ways of reducing the complexity of the musical surface to see this underlying architecture. This viewpoint highlights the "classical" side of the form (its symmetry) while still shedding light on its highly directed (goal-oriented) Romantic side.

From a thematic standpoint, we will focus more on the material itself, and probably will go into great detail in our labeling of material. This will allow us to classify what is happening musically and trace the way it evolves and how it returns. We will probably go beyond the larger divisions to label small, memorable snippets called *motives*. These motives will allow us to see connections between apparently different tunes. They will also help us see the profusion of ideas that may fly by in the development as being "organically connected" (that is, built from the same musical molecules). Because it highlights directed, progress-oriented change (one of the hallmarks of Romantic music), we can think of this as a highly Romantic way of viewing music. It places more value on parsimony (a desire to account for as much of the piece as possible from the fewest possible generative elements) and development and can somewhat mask the role of symmetry.

Now let's consider a little snippet of a Romantic symphony first movement. Try Beethoven's Fifth Symphony; the so-called "fate" motive (da-da-da-dahhh) is easy to follow and remember. It is typical of motives in that you keep redefining it as you go: Is it a specific set of four notes; three notes followed by another note, a third lower; three repeated notes followed by a different pitch; or just short, short, short, long? In some ways, the motive can be any of those things as long as you can hear a connection between the germ-idea and its current form. The overall description of the piece that comes from this sort of listening should be very familiar from program notes and music appreciation texts: "And then the so-and-so enters picking up the such-and-such element from the third horn's this-and-that, etc."

If you've had any training in formal analysis, it most likely was in this Germanic viewpoint. The American classical musical tradition was to a large degree a German transplant and most of the music being analyzed is Germanic as well, so this makes sense. But, as we mentioned above, there is another way to look at things.

Listen to the "Danse Sacrale" from Stravinsky's *Rite of Spring* and try to remember a few of the little modules that keep coming back. Notice how, in spite of the asymmetries, the driving pulse helps everything hang together. A few simple units keep swinging around so they can be seen in different contexts almost from different angles (now elongated, now shortened). You could almost think of this movement as a sort of musical equivalent of a very big Calder mobile. While the music certainly drives us forward, it is hard to think of it as developing: transforming from one thing *into* another. I will not go through a detailed presentation of how these modules interact in the piece, because it is a singular structure, not a widely used form like sonata form. I chose a first example for this nondevelopmental view from a piece that is musically, historically, and geographically ill-suited to the more familiar (Germanic, Romantic, developmental, thematic) mode of analysis to help clarify my meaning. The developmental and nondevelopmental views can be informative in all sorts of works from all sorts of places and times, however.

Blanche Selva, a pianist who taught at the Scuola Cantorum in Paris, wrote this about the sonata form:

> In the sonata, where tonality can be compared to the place of the action, the themes are the characters possessing word, gesture and movement within it. The rhythm is the gesture and the melody the word. The characters or themes all converge, by their gestures or words, in the general action, which is the work. Through interpretation, the character-theme should be presented from the start, with all the habitual rapidity of gestures, the timbre of the voice, the accent of the speech.[1]

While this view certainly allows for development, it doesn't require it. In fact, if we look back at a lot of older music (Couperin suites, for example) we can view the music as a series of character pieces that are lovely but don't necessarily add up to some grand edifice. Moreover, this characteristic is not necessarily a failure.

Development is generally thought of as a virtue in music (or at least in music appreciation classes), so you might be unsure how a nondevelopmental work could be equally meaningful. Part of the problem is that terms like "development" mean so many different things to different people. In a strictly musical sense, let's just think of development as directed change or transformation. Directionality is the key feature: We move from one state toward another. But lots of wonderful things are not directional. Jerry Seinfeld and Larry David of *Seinfeld* fame had a motto, "No hugging, no learning," which could also serve as a motto for many nondevelopmentally oriented composers, even perhaps for Debussy. Beautiful (or funny) ideas need not all be transformed into one organic, inevitable package. Return could be a prod for memory (like Proust's madeleine) without being a triumphal revelation of the second theme now in its true home-key or some other inevitable achievement.

While I have been trying to suggest that either of these approaches could be applied to almost any work, you will sometimes be frustrated by this approach. There are works whose conception is so entangled with one or the other view that trying to look at them with a contrarian's spirit may be like looking for figurative objects in a Jackson Pollock painting; perhaps it is possible, but it's beside the point.

Adopting the wrong approach may blind you to the virtues of the piece you are hearing. More developmental pieces may seem square, repetitive, and blocky if you don't follow the "discourse." More nondevelopmental works may seem static or merely decorative if all you are searching for are developmental transformations of material.

So the problem remains: What should you do while listening attentively? It's almost impossible to pay attention to something without developing expectations, but what kind of expectations should you form and how should you feel when your expectations are defied? This problem becomes particularly acute with contemporary art, where there is nothing like a consensus among artists. You must practically know the specific work already if you are going to have any chance of developing realistic expectations. I think, however, there are ways of developing a framework that is general enough to help you pay attention to what you hear and the subjective affects it causes, without trying to force works into boxes that will impede your ability to discover novel ideas.

It might be helpful to think of a piece as having three aspects:

CONTENT   AFFECT   FORM

These are not separate things, but they can profitably be looked at independently. Content is the aspect that varies most from work to work. Form and affect are very much influenced by human memory and cultural experience, so, though they vary, they often have the commonalities we have mentioned: contrasts, continuities, repetitions, developments, juxtaposition, surprise, closure, tension, drive, lyricism, and so on.

I've said that we must be skeptical of the value that semantic labels bring, but within this current framework at least a little jargon might be helpful:

Content

Content is what we study most often when we first start to look at music; content is what happens at each moment of the piece, like the vocabulary, sentence structure, and the plot or character elements of a novel. Let's look at a few specific kinds of content that are most important for music.

Harmony is generally the combined sound of the notes being played simultaneously. It might be more useful, however, to think of harmony as the element of content that is critical for generating the affect of tension. Harmonies are one of the best devices composers have for creating varying degrees of tension and closure. Even without specialized labels for various sorts of sounds it is easy to hear how the combined harmonic color can make a music unsettled or calm, and so on.

Cadences (strong to weak) operate much like punctuation in text, except that there are many more gradations of finality. They are achieved musically both melodically (think of the way a line can slow down and descend at the end of a phrase) and harmonically (by resolving a tense chord to a stable one). Take any classical piece and every time you hear a break or an ending to a phrase or a section of a phrase, a cadence has occurred.

Structural *highpoints* of a work are critical to determining an overall shape; mapping out these highpoints can reveal much about how a piece is structured. By simply following the increases and decreases in energy and tension it is possible to achieve a real sense of the shape of a work, regardless of any specific formal analytical terms.

We've already defined *motive*; in some works it is a critical element of the material.

Texture is the specific way the musical elements are structured (e.g., a melody with accompaniment, multiple independent lines, thick chords, unison lines) in terms of general configuration. Texture is critical to our perception of any music. The same musical elements arranged in different textures can have greatly different affects.

Affect

Although many kinds of affect are very personal, many others are more objective: a sense of closure, surprise, satisfaction, boredom, and so on. As we've mentioned, even the more ineffable affects contain aspects that can be discussed. Although, as with the sunset, we cannot define the whole issue, we may still be able to clarify aspects of these qualia.

Form

Because form is created through content and the affects it produces, one might wonder what it really is and how it's generated. We've talked about some of the most basic devices:

Repetition: exact or varied
Development: directed change
Expectation: fulfillment or frustration

In real pieces, form has a richness and complexity that would require an entire volume to even begin discussing in any depth. Form can allow the sum of the moments within a piece to be vastly more meaningful than each moment in isolation could ever be. The building blocks with which these complex affects are achieved, however, need not be much more complicated than the simple examples given above (e.g., a fulfilled expectation that comes after a long series of frustrated ones is very different than an immediately fulfilled or frustrated expectation — with each frustrated expectation, the weight placed on the next expectation increases). It is not so much the complexity of individual formal devices as the rich network of relationships between these devices that generates formal complexity.

In order to apply our observations in any of these three categories, we should combine these semantic notions with our perceived affects through the intensional stance we discussed earlier. Simple cases are obvious. Why are interior cadences weaker than the final cadence? To keep the piece moving forward with an incomplete sensation then grant closure in the final cadence. The specific techniques of weakening those cadences are not so important and will change from one stylistic period to the next, but the musical functions will not. A sense of completeness or incompleteness is pretty close to universal even if some musical styles elect to project a sense of infinity by never achieving that closure.

Certain more concrete structural principles occur again and again, like alternations of slower and faster music. More generally, contrast and continuity seem like important affects that can be achieved with devices like repetition (exact or varied), juxtaposition, and so on. Even certain gross emotional shapes are a part of vastly many pieces: slow and melancholy; fast and joyous; tense and driven; lyrical, and so on. I don't mean to reduce the richness of a real musical experience through the banality of these labels. It is important to point out, however, these ways that we can engage with what we're hearing — not with a set of theoretical labels that we have been taught we should find.

There are two possible interpretations of the common complaint made by many listeners, "I just don't get that piece." First, they may have expectations when listening to music that the piece in question does not fulfill. Second, the piece may sound like gibberish — it may seem completely random to that listener, like a cat walking on a piano. The cure for the first ill is finding a way to free yourself from a single listening style, and the solution to the second is probably forcing yourself to listen more or more closely (see my earlier description of the

"Chinese Food Effect"). In either case, though, not getting it is not about how much music theory you have studied. Music theory may help you understand how music does something, but understanding the music itself does not, at its most important level, involve that sort of semantic knowledge. When you have listened thoroughly, often, and well there are ways not to like a piece, but no way not to "get" it. Music, ultimately, is made for what it does in a human mind, not on a piece of paper or in a scholarly article. You might not get how the lungs oxygenate the blood, but you wouldn't be here if you didn't get breathing.

8

DESIGNING MUSIC FOR HUMAN BEINGS

We are musicians and our model is sound not literature, sound not mathematics, sound not theatre, visual arts, quantum physics, geology, astrology or acupuncture.

— Gérard Grisey

We ought not to forget that we still must account for the tones actually sounding, again and again, and shall have no rest from them nor from ourselves — especially from ourselves, for we are the searchers, the restless, who will not tire before we have found out — we shall have no rest, as long as we have not solved the problems that are contained in tones. We may indeed always be barred from actual attainment of this goal. But more certainly, we shall have no rest before we do; the searching spirit will not stop pursuing these problems until it has solved them, solved them in a way that comes as close as anyone can to actual solution. I think, then, contrary to the point of view of those who take indolent pride in the attainments of others and hold our system to be the ultimate, the definitive musical system — contrary to that point of view, I think we stand only at the beginning. We must go ahead!

— Arnold Schoenberg

In this chapter, I will offer my more specific, personal views about how I and a particular group of composers attempt to write music that corresponds to the limits on musical languages and musical meaning discussed in the last two chapters. This is the "how" question of the dialogue I imagined in the prelude: How can a modern composer hope to make a meaningful addition to an impossibly exalted corpus? Up until this point I've tried to argue in a somewhat general and abstract way about art and music, but this chapter will deal more specifically with contemporary composers, compositions, and techniques to serve as a case study of a possible application in artistic works of the ideas I have been discussing theoretically.

The focus in this chapter will shift somewhat, from the audience's perspective to the composer's, to illustrate how artists explore the sort of aesthetic design space that I discussed earlier. This viewpoint is perhaps more familiar in the world of visual arts, where curators have long oriented their expositions around design space explorations whether tacitly or explicitly (e.g., placing late Medieval and early Renaissance works in a way that highlights the emergence of perspective in the representations; placing Impressionist, then Fauvist, then abstract landscapes in a way that highlights a deepening preoccupation with light and color at the expense of "realistic" depiction). It is, of course, equally possible to construct concert programs around the gradual evolution of some aspect of musical practice; however, this is much less frequently done, therefore discussing music in this way may seem less familiar. Yet if I am to have any chance at convincing you to support the kind of art we have been discussing, it is essential that you get a feel for how this art might continue to develop without simply transforming into something entirely abstract and unperceivable. I need to give you a very small peek inside the workings of a living composer's mind, and because I only have access to my own head, that will have to do. Some parts of this chapter may be a bit difficult for those with little or no experience in this domain, and some readers may want to skim the parts that are too difficult to follow. I would, however, recommend to everyone that they try to listen to some of the works and composers I discuss in this chapter, in concert or at least on recordings.

Let's ask it again: How can a composer hope to make a meaningful addition to an impossibly exalted corpus? The first step in finding a solution is to acknowledge that there is a fundamental dilemma at the center of new art music: Even if you believe that basic cognitive principles allow novel musical languages to be created, when is a listener supposed to learn these new languages? Even the most adventurous or committed among us will have relatively few occasions to hear new composers' works. The pieces we do hear will often not be available in recorded format and will not be played again anywhere near us for years to come. This indisputable reality makes many wonder whether it is necessary to deviate so greatly from our existing musical models, because many listeners have already learned those languages. I suspect that some of these doubters are unsure of even the theoretical possibility of creating something meaningful that is not essentially similar — in not just deep ways, but also more evident ways — to our tonal models (most music critics fall into this category).

I have suggested in earlier chapters that I think this *is* possible: A composer can use the first principles deciphered through studying the music and sound humans generate and process to create something very different from what we have known before, but possessing equal potential as a musical language. The bulk of this book has been my attempt to answer why, if possible, this might be worthwhile, or even important. Now what remains to be attempted is offering an answer to how a composer might try to do this.

In the final analysis, general theoretical observations will not be worth much unless artists are able to figure out a concrete way of using them to make real works of art. We must discuss the hard, specific and personal "Here's how I ..." at this point and not the general "How might one... ?" Although I could try to analyze certain works I find successful (and will do so to a small degree), I fear that would be too specific. So, instead, I would like to try putting forward the way that I, and some of the contemporary composers I most admire, attempt to answer this question when we sit down to work each day. Because I have been part of a small movement, I will try to focus on the movement as a whole so that I do not descend too far into personal specificity and self-justification. For the purpose of our discussion, the utility of the compositional approach I will present does not depend on whether I'm right; what really counts is the quality of music these attitudes allow me, or others, to produce. And in the context of this book, what is really important is to show one possible framework for responses to the dilemmas facing the creation of the sort of new, difficult art (the reception of which) we have been discussing up to this point: one possible "how." Although you may reject my conclusions, I think that looking at one way a group of composers might try to solve these problems in artistic works can perhaps convert a somewhat bleak assessment of the current situation for art into the groundwork for attempts to go ahead. At the very least, it ought to show that the very difficult set of constraints that face a composer today are not completely irreconcilable.

I need to offer one major caveat before we begin in earnest. When I move away from my work table and start to look at music as an observer, it seems obvious that a whole range of solutions to the problems inherent in composing a piece are possible. This is the detached reasoning of an outside observer, however. When I'm in the heat of the moment making the actual decisions that let me create a piece of music, I am incapable of taking this broad perspective. Intellectually, I may be sure that there are many potentially successful responses to a given set of compositional problems, and that my own is just one possibility; however, on a gut level, I can't really believe in those other solutions (at least not while I'm still writing the piece). To create effectively, I think you need to be certain, not just pretty sure. Artists may be wracked with doubt about whether they have achieved their aims, but I don't believe they can be effective if they doubt those aims.

All this is my way of saying that you will get the sense in this chapter that I'm awfully sure I'm right and everyone else is wrong, because this is the way I need to think when writing my music. I want you to get a glimpse of the way a set of composers see the world and how that shapes their work. In a certain sense I could probably have chosen a different set of composers with a somewhat different outlook to demonstrate something very similar, but it would be a view from outside.

Therefore I decided to risk the danger of this seeming too much like self-justification in order to offer a more direct and personal view of how at least a few composers try to make their music.

So, we return to our question once again: How can someone set off, without a map, on a quest for the compositional "grail" of really new music that possesses the same potential for aesthetic richness as the greatest tonal music? Every day when I sit down to compose I think about this question, and every day I have to feel sure that I have found some kind of answer in order to continue. You might think of the way I, and several others, try to create musical structures that are both novel and "comprehensible" to human listeners as the "spectral approach." This approach is built around the idea that writing music is not just pushing around tunes, intervals, numbers, or harmonies; it is designing evolutions of sound in time to be processed by human beings listening attentively.

The Spectral Approach

The spectral approach looks beyond the specifics of tonal music for the more general rules that allowed tonality to function so well. The idea behind this approach can perhaps be most clearly explained through an analogy: Engineers who have built fantastically complex devices through successive refinements of existing apparatuses sometimes hit a roadblock. In this case, the scientific method tells them to go back to the basic theories that allowed the initial device to function and reconsider them. It is often the case that a new consideration of these same "first principles" can lead to a very different perspective. Continued progress may depend upon the use of an entirely different apparatus to accomplish the same underlying function. This was the approach adopted by the spectralists starting in the early 1970s with the French composers Gérard Grisey and Tristan Murail.

Spectral composers felt that much new music was not producing satisfactory results: The theoretical constructions that were being discussed at great length by the composers of the time did not seem to correspond to anything audible in the actual works. In their reflections about a basis for musical construction that would function, be audible, and not return to tonality, they saw only one realm in which to explore: sound. Even the earliest Western treatises about music have used sound as the underpinning for their theoretical constructions — long before any deep understanding of acoustical or psychoacoustical principles existed. This recognizes the indisputable reality that human hearing is not primarily *for* music and therefore music must be designed *for* hearing. Theorists have always regarded musical hearing as a secondary, nonindependent effect of our general capacity for hearing. Nonetheless, phenomena affecting our general hearing (such as the combination of multiple partials into a unified sense of pitch) have clear implications both for musical and for environmental sounds. This is not to suggest that hearing can dictate a musical style, but rather that a study of sound and hearing can elucidate the borders within which a valid (from the perceptual point of view) style might be created (the contours of some region in the design space we discussed earlier).

Clearly, the extended relations of tonality were not "natural" in any meaningful sense, but they were developed from models that, just as surely, were (the opposition of consonance and dissonance, the hierarchy of tension between intervallic relations played by instruments with complex timbres, etc.). Twentieth-century composers who speculated that consonance and dissonance were purely cultural, and that one could create a music where the fifths were dissonant and the minor seconds consonant, were simply wrong. While many aspects of most musical traditions are learned (through context and exposure), we can only learn to hear things that do not too directly contradict our natural intuitions.[1] Like the king in *The Little Prince*, composers who wish to command the stars must be careful only to order the sun to rise in the morning and set at night, because we are severely lacking in the means to alter that arrangement significantly.

Spectral composers have sought to create a music that was built to function (by function, I mean to create specific, *compositionally controlled* auditory impressions in the listener's subjective awareness), instead of a music that functions in spite of how it was built. For example, some of the classic pieces from the Darmstadt era of serialism in the 1950s and 1960s — such as Luigi Nono's *Il Canto Sospeso* or Pierre Boulez's *Le Marteau sans maitre* — whose effectiveness derives from a sense of orchestration, motion, and contrast, not through a study of the voluminous analyses of permutations and calculations that went into their composition. The pieces work *in spite* of this intellectual baggage not *because* of it. Therefore, the spectralists turned to the developing fields of acoustics, psychoacoustics, electronic and computer music, and cognitive sciences to find directly things that *could* be heard and impressions that *could* be created. This information did not tell them how to compose, but merely where to look.

I will try in this chapter to give a general guide and orientation to spectral music. However, just as a study of overtones, temperaments, and formal models (while useful) does not clearly define Mozart's style, I cannot really "explain" spectral music, but can offer background and perspective for further study and listening. Real musical understanding is sensory. Ultimately the real "meaning" of the music lies in the feeling of rightness, surprise, beauty, tension, or whatever else the music produces. The real ideas of the music are musical in nature and no amount of conceptual description should be accepted as a substitute for "the tones actually sounding." Nonetheless, we must address the question I'm sure you are all ready to ask: What is spectral music?

What Is Spectral Music?

As I've said, formulating a clear definition of a broad musical category like spectral music is nearly impossible. Only through extended familiarity not just with a type of music, but also with its milieu, can one hope to develop meaningful categories that are more than mere simplified labels. Thus, I will try to describe a mixture of historical and musical developments that together have helped define the spectral school. I'll also include a few very targeted "analytical" examples interspersed within the discussion.[2] These examples will be very broad in nature and are really intended for those readers who have little or no experience with this music. All the examples are drawn from works that are available on commercial CDs, and hopefully some of them will incite you to hear the pieces themselves. While my definition of spectral music is a personal one, its broad outlines are largely undisputed. As with any definition, however, many of its specific details are controversial and many of those to whom this label would be appropriate do not like being classified. In any case, for the present discussion what really matters is the general outline.

Spectral music developed as a school of composition in the early seventies inspired by the works of two composers, Tristan Murail and Gérard Grisey. Its composers now cover three compositional generations and a large variety of styles. They write for all types of instrumental groupings and often take advantage of new technological possibilities for enriching their musical palettes. The musical approach is profoundly different from both structuralist (postserial) approaches and hybrid (neo-Romantic or postmodern) aesthetics; however, the pieces remain intimately linked to the interpretive tradition of Western instrumental music. While tape pieces have been written by some spectral composers, their goal is not electro-acoustic music, but rather a new type of instrumental music with different sounds, textures, and evolutions.

The term spectral music was coined by Hugues Dufourt,[3] but the most pertinent remark for understanding its meaning was made by Tristan Murail during his lectures at the 1980 Darmstadt summer course. He referred to spectral composition as an attitude toward music and composition, rather than a set of techniques. While that remark was made without elaboration, it offers a useful starting point for our investigation of what spectral music is.

Spectral music addresses broad aesthetic consequences instead of specific stylistic ones. Thus, spectral composers can have vastly different styles and some even prefer to reject the label. However, all of these composers share a central belief that music is ultimately sound evolving in time. Viewing music in this way, as a special case of the general phenomenon of sound, facilitates these composers' use of the available knowledge in the fields of acoustics and psychoacoustics within their music. They can refine their understanding of what sound is, how it may be controlled, and what, ultimately, a listener will be able to perceive. That knowledge, when applied musically, provides powerful new compositional tools. Musical works may be conceived much more closely to the manner in which they will ultimately be perceived than would otherwise be possible. Sounds and musical colors (timbres) can be sculpted in time to produce musical effects. The panoply of methods and techniques needed to create these effects and to manipulate sound in this way is secondary. They are simply the means of achieving a sonic end and not a discourse with intellectual pretensions in its own right.

Combining and manipulating spectral materials in the same abstract ways in which intervallic materials are treated (without taking into account the precise nature of these materials and a listener's perceptual capacities) does not yield music that I would classify as spectral. Spectral composers have often, in fact, chosen points of departure or made use of materials that are not directly related to sonic phenomena. The manner in which a spectral composer treats and develops his or her material, however, constantly takes into consideration the sonic entity that is being generated. This is what Grisey really meant when he wrote that our model is sound. It is not that a composer cannot take inspiration from "visual arts, quantum physics, geology, astrology or acupuncture"; in fact, Grisey wrote one piece inspired by the painter Piero della Francesca and another inspired by a pulsar, but I don't think he was just a hypocrite. Sound is the model for spectral composers in the same way that light is the model for Impressionist painters, yet Monet did not simply paint luminous washes of color. In Monet's series of paintings of the Rouen cathedral at different times of day, it is clear that the proximate subject (the cathedral) is just a vehicle for communicating the real content: light, shadow, and color. This is what Grisey means: The real content of music is not mathematics, quantum physics, or even aesthetic philosophy, but sound, the way sound changes in time and the affects it produces in the human mind.

This may seem like an obvious idea to anyone who was not a composer in the twentieth century, but to those of us who were, this was a major breakthrough. The prevailing schools of composition either regarded music as the structured combination of musical symbols (notes, rhythms, dynamics, etc.), with an emphasis on the interest or complexity of these structures; or as a vehicle for conceptual ideas (in parallel with the conceptual movements in visual arts we discussed earlier). In more recent years, new trends have also emerged that refer back to a more romantic notion that regards music as being essentially a vehicle for emotional content — usually produced through references (literal or evocative) to past works already possessing cultural associations. Yet in any of these cases the piece at its most essential level is something other than sounds heard in time by human listeners, and this is the fundamental belief of spectral composers. Any other ideas (brilliant or insipid) will be useful or not only in how they affect those sounds and the mental representations they create in listeners; they have no independent justification.

A score created by a composer with this spectral attitude serves simply as a means of communicating the composer's sonic intentions to the musicians. The score is not the actual musical work, and any notational or other innovations that may be present in spectral scores are attempts to express the composer's intent more clearly with regard to final realizations; the actual piece of music *is* what the sonic realization becomes in the mind of a human listener.

Because neither the technical manipulations used to generate and manipulate the musical material, nor the procedural means of notating the score are central or indispensable to spectral composition (these aspects are in fact in constant mutation), we must instead return to Murail's observation that, in fact, spectral music is neither about techniques nor styles but, at its core, is simply a question of attitude. This doesn't mean that a spectral composer does not need to have technique. In fact, writing this sort of music is often very technically demanding, and a lack of technique may well cause the piece to fail. Spectral composers do not believe, however, that the success or interest of the piece on technical terms is a justification or validation of the musical work. In whatever manner it was made, the work must ultimately succeed "independently."

A great advantage of viewing the problems of musical organization from the perspective of the broader category of sonic organization is that very successful models already exist. Some of the best sets of models for sound organization are the instruments that have evolved over time into sound generators that composers want to use and listeners want to hear. Thus, it is not surprising that some of the first important spectral pieces made use of instrumental models in creating their orchestral sonorities. You may not think of an individual instrumental note as a particularly complex or rich model for music; it might seem like some tiny indifferent musical atom. However, each and every instrumental note, in fact, contains a very complex interior structure that constantly changes in time — as complex in its own way as a piece of composed music. This is why so many synthetic sounds have an "artificial" sheen to them — they lack this interior mobility and are thus perceived as too simple or static by our ears. It is extraordinarily difficult to generate an artificial sound with the richness of internal structure that most natural sounds already possess.[4] For acoustic instruments, builders have sought to use the physical properties of vibrating materials to create sounds that are at once extremely appealing in their richness and sufficiently coherent in their structure to be usable as elements within larger structures like chords (multiple notes played simultaneously by one or more instruments).

Of course, to listeners much of this richness exists at a level too microscopic to hear. We perceive the sound globally as brassy, reedy, bright, or somber; we perceive its pitch, its loudness, and so on. We would certainly notice the lack of complex internal structure, but we are not consciously aware of the details of that structure and the way they influence our global perceptions (any more than we perceive the atomic motion that gives rise to temperature in the air around us). With the advent of electronic devices that decompose sounds into their constituent elements, however, we could begin to see the workings of these structures. This internal organization offered a new model for how a large number of elements might evolve together in ways that offer both juxtaposition and collaboration within a larger structure.

In Gérard Grisey's first pieces, he used a close-up view of this structure as the model for much larger orchestral structures, sometimes even complete sections. Grisey liked to describe the process as "putting a microscope on the sound."[5] His idea was not to recreate the original sound (which he could have just played, after all), but to make something new that preserves the overall coherence that comes from being part of a unified acoustical structure at a larger level. This may sound a bit puzzling, but there is a very good parallel in the visual arts. The painter Chuck Close has made a career of painting realistic representative paintings where the picture is pixilated into individually visible shapes and colors. Each spot in the picture has a definite size and shape while still giving its overall color and shading characteristics to the larger image, which becomes clear once you step back from the canvas to view it. The total is definitely something more or at least different from a photographic reproduction. The difference between Close's paintings and these first works of Grisey is that the end result in the musical use need not remain photorealistic to even a moderate degree; it has to preserve just enough of the structure of the model to maintain its dual nature: as a fused global sound and as the sum of multiple individual sounds. The musically inclined may notice that this model is used in a parallel manner to the use of tonal harmony within late-Baroque counterpoint; this is an example of convergent musical evolution. This musical technique of using the interior structure of a sound as a model for a rich new orchestral object, transforming its micro-fluctuations into macro-forms, is called "orchestral synthesis."

Let's look briefly at an example of this orchestral synthesis from one of Grisey's pieces, *Partiels* (1975), for eighteenth instruments. I'm going to include some music notation in this example, because it is fairly simple and it should be easy to follow the shapes, even for those who do not read music. For the later examples, I'll try to do as much as possible with descriptions. *Partiels* is one of the best-known and earliest examples of a composer using an instrumental analysis to create a harmonic and gestural model that is then realized by an instrumental ensemble. Personal computers were, of course, not an option for Grisey at the time that he wrote the piece, so he used an electronic sonogram device to analyze the attack of a low E2 (an octave and a sixth below middle-C) played loudly on the trombone. The analysis of this attack became the model for the opening gesture of the piece (this gesture is then repeated with increasing degrees of alteration throughout the first section of the piece).

While the specific analyses and devices he used are no longer available, we can very easily approximate the steps Grisey took with current tools. The first step is the generation of a sonogram showing the attack of the low E on a trombone played forte.

Notice that the sound is made of component bands (called partials) that are equidistant on the frequency axis. This is because the sound is "harmonic" like most pitched sounds (the partials are located at integer multiples of the fundamental frequency that determines the pitch of the sound). If we look at the way the loudness of the partials changes in time, we can use the darkness of each band to see that the partials enter one after the other with lower partials generally entering earlier and

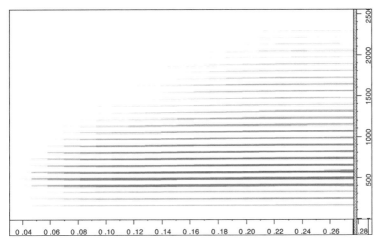

Figure 8.1 A sonogram showing the low E on a trombone played forte. The x-axis shows the time, the y-axis shows frequency in Hz, and the darkness shows amplitude.

higher partials appearing later. We should also notice that the lowest partials — including the fundamental — are not the darkest (loudest) ones; the fifth and ninth partials are louder. This is especially interesting because both of these partials form dissonant high-tension intervals with the fundamental. These loud dissonant partials give the aggressive, brassy quality to the trombone sound. Finally, we can observe that the partials above this louder region gradually trail off in amplitude.

If we want to use this information in an instrumental score, we will have to translate it from the domains of time, frequency, and amplitude to more musical dimensions like pitch dynamic and rhythm. This will often require approximations to the nearest available values that we call "quantification." By quantifying this sonogram, we can generate a

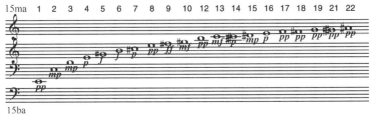

Figure 8.2 A musical model that corresponds to the partials of the harmonic series (approximated to the nearest quarter-tone). The numbers above the top staff represent the partial rankings within the harmonic series.

musical model that corresponds to the partials of the harmonic series. When this is transcribed into musical notation of pitches (approximated to the nearest quarter-tone) and dynamics, the series in figure 8.2 is produced. This series, coupled with a rhythmic modeling of the successive entrance of the partials, can then be used to produce the instrumental score.[6]

In the following excerpt from the final score, Grisey wrote the partial ranking next to each note. While it is generally not very helpful to write a textual commentary on the effect of a musical passage, I think it is important to note how striking this moment is. At the very start of the piece one hears the trombone attack forte, with the double bass repeating the attacking gesture with less and less determination. This allows the sound of the sustained trombone to gradually emerge. Just as this happens, the sustained note that has been performing a decrescendo begins to give way — through a cross-fade — to an instrumentally synthesized imitation of itself. This instrumental timbre does not seek to present an indistinguishable copy of the original, but rather to generate an amplification and transfiguration of the trombone note. The listener can still sense the underlying trombone color of the sound, while at the same time a doorway is opened up to a vast new domain of sound found within the original sound. Deploying these notes in a vastly stretched out imitation of a trombone does not really sound like a trombone; it sounds like something entirely new, while preserving a distinct trombone-color in its overall presentation. It also creates an orchestral entrance that sounds neither like a chord nor like a single sound, but that manages to simultaneously possess many elements of both.

This particular musical moment, especially at the time it happened, was to have an enormous impact. Many of the second- and third-generation spectral composers have cited their first hearing of *Partiels* as having caused their initial interest in the musical potential of sonic phenomena.

Another defining piece of the spectral movement is Tristan Murail's *Gondwana*. The brief opening section of this piece for large orchestra is a series of enormous, orchestrally synthesized bell sounds that are gradually transformed into an orchestrally synthesized brass sound. Again, the idea is not to offer a realistic simulation; after all, Murail could have just included bells with his orchestra. The idea is to go inside of

Figure 8.3 Excerpt from the opening of Grisey's *Partiels* with the composer's annotations of the partial ranking of each note. © 1976 by CASA RICORDI — BMG RICORDI SpA. Used with permission.

a bell sound and render audible the normally microscopic structures that make it beautiful. Moreover, by recreating a hybrid with bell-like properties, it is possible to gradually manipulate these structures and make musical objects less and less bell-like in gradual increments (doing this with real bells would at least require a foundry).

One way to create this effect would have been to analyze acoustic bells and then analyze a brass instrument, but by looking at distinct objects like that it is quite difficult to create a convincing intermediate space between the bell and brass sounds. So Murail turned to the developing world of electronic synthesis. A few years earlier a researcher and composer at Stanford, John Chowning, had published the description of a versatile and simple technique for sound synthesis based on frequency modulation. (This is like the vibrato of a string instrument, but instead of vibrating seven or eight times a second the vibrato might cycle hundreds of times per second.) This technique became the basis of the Yamaha DX-7, one of the first really successful digital synthesizers. For Murail, however, this technique offered a single method, which when used as a model could generate both convincing bells and brass spectra.

Murail used a simplified form of this FM-synthesis model (one that did not take the relative loudness of the partials into account) and constructed a bell sound and a brass sound using the same carrier frequency but different modulators. He then chose three other modulators that produced sonorities with intermediate sonic properties. In all this series of five carriers affected by a single modulator produces five different modulation-based harmonies that are played by the orchestra. In the piece, these chords are completed by other chords that were generated by calculating intermediate steps (interpolations) between some of these FM chords.[7]

There is more to a bell sound than a set of pitches, however. There is also the way those pitches function in time. Unlike brass instruments, bell sounds have a very sharp attack, meaning that all the partials sound immediately. In fact, these partials are completed by a brief spurt of noise called the "attack transient." What then happens is the gradual disappearance of the partials moving from high to low, until only the fundamental of the bell (called the "drone") remains. In the opening passage of *Gondwana*, Murail wants to move from a bell-like orchestral sound toward a brasslike one, so the overall shape of the orchestral gesture is gradually transformed as can be seen in figure 8.4.

I have given quite simplistic descriptions of the Grisey and Murail passages; the music in question is in fact much more complex. By focusing on one very prominent aspect, however, I hope to give a clear handle on some of the basic ways spectral composers have tried to integrate sonic models into musical processes. These sort of literal models never represented the totality of a piece or even a section of a piece, but they were very important to the early spectral works and can still be found

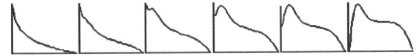

Figure 8.4 The overall shape of the orchestral gesture as it transforms from a bell-like sound to a brasslike sound in the opening section of Tristan Murail's *Gondwana*.

in new pieces; however, a more complex and sometimes less direct sort of model is now more common.

Examples of this more subtle type of model can be found in any of Grisey's or Murail's pieces after the mid-seventies. However, I'd like to illustrate this more complex use of models with one of my own pieces, «*Receuil de pierres et de sable…*». In this piece, I had many different categories of models ranging from the purely poetical, through statistical behaviors, all the way to fully concrete. This work is scored for two harps tuned a quarter-tone apart and an ensemble of six instruments. Together, the two harps create a sort of microtonal super harp that can play parts one harp is not capable of performing. The other six instruments create something like a sounding board for the two harps. The sonic/instrumental analogy at the heart of the piece is drawn from the piano.

Sounds produced by the piano have two distinct characteristics: the percussive attack produced by the hammers and the long sustain produced by the cast-iron sounding board and facilitated by a sustain pedal that allows the dampers to be lifted and the strings left free to vibrate. Of course, because I'm only using the piano's hammers and soundboard metaphorically, the nondirect nature of the analogy opens up many possibilities. The sustaining instruments of the ensemble can draw out the notes attacked by the harps, but they can also change and color them. This is a malleable sort of resonant body.

This technical or logistical analogy is inspired by a more poetic analogy: the raking of the sand in Zen gardens. I was drawn to the idea of the successive passages of the rakes being like successive percussive attacks that leave an ever-richer pattern on the sand or in the ensemble. All of this leads to the point where the raking, or playing of new attacks, becomes less important and interesting than the design that has been created.

Other types of models appear in the piece that are more specific, closer to the Grisey and Murail examples that we've already discussed. At three pivotal points, the ensemble recreates through orchestral synthesis the sound of a Japanese mouth organ called a *sho*. The specificity of these three moments could be thought of as somewhat akin to the boulders encrusted in the sand/ocean of a Zen garden. The piece also uses what I would describe as behavioral models in the central solo for

two flutes (accompanied by the harps). For this solo, I analyzed a Japanese flute called a *Ryuteki*. This flute is basically a tube (like all flutes)
made of smoked bamboo, but it has a small lead tube with a different
diameter between its head joint and its body. The story is that a flutist broke his flute on the way to the concert and had to repair the flute
quickly, producing this instrument. Anecdotes aside, this flute has a
very strange doubleness to its sound because the oscillating air (called
"standing waves") in the two tubes with different diameters and lengths
interfere and interact with each other. The way this doubleness occurs
is very specific, yielding certain intervals in its spectrum and producing
certain melodic configurations when a flutist changes pitch by increasing the force and speed of his or her breath. In the central solo for the
two flutes, I mimicked this behavior with two Western flutes. Though
many of the gestures and sounds these two flutes communally produce
come straight from Ryuteki analyses, I could take this "instrument"
into speeds, registers, and harmonic areas a real Ryuteki, with its more
limited key system, could never go.

One has to take these very limited examples with a grain of salt; in
each case I have dealt with only one or two aspects of a much richer
musical situation. Moreover, even if I were to give many more examples and spend much more time describing them, they would remain
an incomplete way of understanding the attitude. Any summary affir-
mations that I might make about a spectral style are all both true and
false. I might assert that the music has made color into a central element
of the musical discourse, often elevating it to the level of the principal
narrative thread; or that orchestral fusion is often a main feature of its
surface texture, so that individual voices are subsumed in the richness
of the overall texture and color; or that the basic sonic image is often
sonorous and resonant, giving the music a sort of acoustic glow that
comes from the coherence — in the domain of frequencies — of the
different constituent pitches; or even that this music simply sounds profoundly different from other musics. While examples could be found
to support all of these attributes, counterexamples could certainly be
found. Spectral composers have produced music that is too diverse for
any kind of blanket assertion to be true. The only true constant for
composers like me is that we consider music ultimately to *be* sound, not

symbols or concepts, and see composition as the sculpting in time[8] of those sounds that a listener will hear. If we can only go so far in a book like this with technical/musical examples, however, perhaps we ought to enrich the ideas with a little more general and historical context.

Where Did Spectral Music Come From?

Spectral music has always cast itself in the role of a revolutionary movement, fighting against the academicism (in the French sense)[8] and dogma they perceived in the French New Music scene of the seventies. And while this revolutionary stance does reflect the reality of the movement's emergence as a counterweight to the postserialists surrounding Pierre Boulez, it does not mean that the movement was purely reactive.

Spectral music does have its compositional forebears. One can certainly cite Edgard Varèse's sensitivity to sound or even the Italian futurists' obsessions with making a new sonic vocabulary for music.[9] Or, more specifically, one might point to André Jolivet's experiments with harmonic spectra (inspired by an attempt to imitate the mixture stops on an organ), or the early microtonal experiments of Ivan Wïshnegradsky or Julián Carrillo, not to mention some of Karlheinz Stockhausen's works.[10] In a certain sense, *Stimmung*, a vocal piece by Stockhausen built around singing different vowels in a fixed harmonic spectrum, is a spectral piece already. And Stockhausen's experiments both there and in his large piece for multiple ensembles, *Gruppen*, were very influential on Grisey, albeit less so on Murail. Per Nørgård's *Voyage into the Golden Screen* (1968) is another example of what might be called a protospectral work, but don't worry if these references don't mean much to you. The point is that many of these ideas were in the air in the 1960s and I wanted to list some names and works for those who might want to listen to some very strange, but quite wonderful, musical experiments.

Although all these influences on the development of the spectral movement were important, in a general way, my focus will be on the three figures who had the most direct impact on the origins of spectral music: Olivier Messiaen, György Ligeti, and Giacinto Scelsi. These three figures played pivotal and very different roles in Grisey and Murail's compositional and aesthetic development. It is difficult to imagine their music of the early seventies — the pieces that have become the defining classics of early spectral music — without the profound influence exerted by all three figures on the young and still searching Grisey and Murail of the late sixties. Don't worry if you've never heard of these composers — I'll try to briefly explain the aspects of their musical thinking that were important to the Spectralists.

Le Maître des Maîtres

Olivier Messiaen was the composer who assisted most directly in the birth of the spectral movement. While his music was probably less influential for spectral composers than that of Ligeti or Scelsi, it was Messiaen who was the professor of both Grisey and Murail. This influence affected not just Grisey and Murail, but a whole group of French composers who formed the group L'Itinéraire with Murail. (L'Intinéraire in its original incarnation was, a composers' collective and performing ensemble that tried to elevate sound and timbre from a decorative role to the center of musical discourse.) These composers (Michaël Levinas, Roger Tessier, Hugues Dufourt, etc.) shared many of the attitudes that would come to be associated with spectral music. Messiaen influenced all of these composers, and through them the spectral movement in several different but very important ways.

Messiaen's most direct influence was the weight that spectralists place on the harmonic dimension of musical composition, as opposed to the emphasis on melodies and the linear (lines) dimensions of music, which had become preeminent in the mid-twentieth century. This aspect of spectral music is often attributed to the traditional French preoccupation with color (think of Fauré or Ravel), but I think that it goes deeper. In the late sixties most European composers, even in France, were still under the thrall of Darmstadtian postserialism, which sought mightily to limit the importance of the vertical dimension of composition (harmony) at all costs.[11] Yet Messiaen, while encouraging his students to adopt this postserial approach (at the time he saw no other "progressive" option, and Messiaen was not one to suggest returning to the past), was also talking to them about the "vraie harmonie" of a piece.

The idea was that really successful music needed to be more than logically coherent, and that some note choices were not just more interesting or complex than others; they were more "right." This idea, which might seem naive to many composers, struck a real chord with the spectralists. As Tristan Murail has said, "I verify the truth of this idea in my work each day, as do all composers who attempt to write a music based on sound."[12]

Messiaen's use of all different sorts of music in his teaching (Greek and Hindu metric systems, Gregorian neumes, well-known and obscure pieces from the repertoire, naturalistic reproductions of birdsong, etc.) and his unconventional analytical methods have been widely documented, but I don't think the effect of this on the early spectral composers has been sufficiently emphasized. Messiaen's highly personal overview of musical ideas, for Grisey, Murail, and others, became an impetus to look for the common links between vastly different manifestations of musical phenomena. The common links they discovered were sonic, not structural, in nature. The use of a wide range of primary sources for sonic inspiration (i.e., gagaku, Höömi singing, bell sounds, speech, etc.) remains an important aspect of much spectral music.

Perhaps the greatest influence that Messiaen exerted on Murail and Grisey was in his role as mentor. Murail has said that in many ways he was not really teaching his students composition, but he was helping them to look into themselves to find what was really authentic. He was ingraining in them the deep sense of integrity to a personal vision that is required to create original art. And more than this, he was there at the perfect moment to say, "the way you've found, that is your path."[13] This may seem a bit mystical or over the top, but this was exactly the sort of encouragement that allowed composers in their early twenties to feel confident enough to forge a path far outside of the mainstream.

External Appearances

The works of György Ligeti from the 1960s played a pivotal role in many spectral composers' efforts to find a means of realizing their vision of a music that sounded and worked differently. In the late '50s, Ligeti spent a few years in the electronic music studio of the German radio. During this time he partially realized three tape pieces. Working with the electronic medium, albeit in a primitive form, he came to think about music in a very different way. He started to think of musical situations and objects as global colors and textures and of counterpoint as the superposition of these layers. He saw new formal possibilities emerge from the techniques of splicing and cross-fades. And most important, he realized that this new approach to sound — which could not have been achieved without his exposure to studio techniques — need not apply only to the electronic medium. The sketches he had made for his second and third electronic pieces were thus transformed into the sketches for his first micropolyphonic orchestral works (*Apparitions 1958–59* and *Atmosphères 1961*).

This may seem like a contradiction: Earlier, I spoke above about how much richer and more complex acoustic sounds are when compared to artificial sounds. Studio techniques are not just questions of the sounds made, however. A host of techniques were developed to manipulate sounds in time. Because these techniques used an electronic and not a physical support, they suggested a range of novel musical processes, from slow cross-fades or fade-outs to infinitely long loops of sound to sudden cuts that let sounds appear or disappear instantly, and so on, which are easy to do with a volume knob or a pair of scissors but much less so with breath or bows.

Ligeti never returned to the electronic medium. He decided that he possessed a greater mastery of the sonic tools offered by traditional instruments and that even his "electronic" ideas might be better realized through these means (in large part because of the greater richness of internal structure I discussed earlier). The resulting works remain some of the most sonically striking works that exist, the entire orchestra becomes a wailing or shining mass that can change its color or density suddenly and produce truly dramatic effects. The basic sound of these works, in a distorted form, should be familiar from Stanley Kubrick's use of tiny out-of-context excerpts from Ligeti's music in his films (most notably in *The Shining* and *2001: A Space Odyssey*). Bowdlerized versions of this music have shown up ever since in horror films, because it is so charged with tension.

Ligeti saw a violin, flute, or clarinet as a tremendously sophisticated sound generator and saw no reason not to use them in the same ways he had tried to use the very rudimentary radio oscillators and other sound-generators of the electronic music world of the 1950s. This crosspollination of ideas let him create instrumental passages that would have been nearly impossible to conceive without the metaphor of electronic music processes. Therefore one can properly speak of Ligeti as a "postelectronic" composer. Ligeti had arrived at a music that, while no longer directly electronic, would have been impossible to create had he not passed through an electronic phase. More broadly, any nonelectronic music whose composition depends on ideas, concepts, or techniques borrowed from the electronic domain can be thought of in this way.

This idea of a postelectronic music that uses instrumental synthesis to simulate electronic sounds with orchestral instruments is clearly central to spectral music. Ligeti's influence, however, goes beyond these conceptual realms. His techniques for achieving orchestral fusion used perceptual saturation. The sheer mass of sound (with its vast number of independently moving lines) forces listeners into a global sort of hearing rather than attempting to follow individual lines. This technique became central to spectral music as did Ligeti's juxtapositions of extreme dissonances and shockingly open consonances as a means of producing contrast. Moreover, his treatment of individual instruments as tone generators within a larger whole (not as real melodic lines) has also all been very influential for spectral composers. In many ways, pieces like *Atmosphères* and *Lontano* are almost trying to be spectral: They present the same high degree of instrumental fusion, the unusual colors, and the slow, almost eventfree unfolding as the early spectral pieces.

Were it not for the severe limitations that Ligeti's dependence on "cluster"-based harmonies (harmonies built out of adjacent semitones) created and the limited scope of the formal processes he employed, it would be easy to imagine him having become a spectral composer.[14] However, Ligeti's harmonic language forced him into constantly choosing between extremes of hyperdissonance or hyperconsonance. His language did not allow for much fertile terrain between these poles. Moreover, his formal analogies with tape-splicing and panel sections also kept him from having much room for a sense of directionality in the musical discourse, which is so important to large-scale musical form. Ligeti seemed keenly aware of these limitations, and I suspect they are the reason that his works from this period are mostly quite short.

Instead of searching for a richer, more powerful harmonic language and more gripping, multifaceted processes of formal development, Ligeti decided to move on. He began by focusing more intensely on motivic gestures (in pieces like *San Francisco Polyphony*) and a few years later had moved so far as to write the unabashedly referential horn trio (*Homage à Brahms*). By this time, his interest for spectral composers had long been lapsed, but the influence of his seminal works of the sixties remains. Even some younger spectral composers (including myself) began their march toward spectral music by following the path that Ligeti had marked during that decade.

Penetrating to the Interior

While many of the surface features of spectral music come from Ligeti (the fused mass movements of sound, the micropolyphonic thickening of textures, the global formal movements, etc.), the sonic content took its inspiration from another source. As we've noted, Ligeti worked with a very constrained harmonic toolkit; this was insufficient for the young Grisey and Murail, who were looking for a way to give harmony back the essential and structural (read: directional) role it had enjoyed in the past. During their "Rome Prize"[15] stays in Italy, both Grisey and Murail came to know the Italian composer Giacinto Scelsi,[16] who is much less well known to the musical public.

Scelsi began his career as a serialist. He studied with Walter Klein, a pupil of Schoenberg, in Vienna and was among the first Italian twelve-tone composers. In the years leading up to the Second World War, he started moving away from serialism. He studied with Egon Koehler, a protégé of Scriabin, and was drawn to Eastern philosophy and mysticism. Scelsi then suffered a breakdown, which led to years of hospitalization (at this time, he had already composed approximately thirty pieces). The story, surely apocryphal but with a grain of truth, is that during his recovery he would spend hours each day banging on single notes of the piano and attempting to listen inside the sound. This was said to have brought him back to the purely sensual relationship with sound he had enjoyed as a child. This approach seemed to liberate him, and in the early fifties he began composing again, but in a very different style. He sought to write a music that penetrated the interior of the sound. As he said, "He who does not penetrate to the interior, to the heart of the sound, even though a perfect craftsman, a great technician, will never be a true artist, a true musician."[17]

During this period, Scelsi composed prolifically, writing nearly a hundred pieces of somewhat varying quality but all focused on this idea of voyaging to the heart of the sound. Perhaps the most extreme and influential piece in this style is his *Quattro Pezzi per Orchestra (Ciascuno su una nota sola)* (Four Pieces for Orchestra [Each one on a single note]). This piece, which is a sort of a prespectral answer to Schoenberg's famous orchestral study in tone-color, "Farben," uses microtonal and orchestrational fluctuations to color the single note (often including its triadlike expansion) that dominates each movement. In this way, music that should seem static opens up a new universe of microlistening[18] and microevents. His concerto for violin, *Anahit,* uses a similar technique; the central note being colored, however, is in constant progression. This imparts a sense of formal progress, or at least formal *process*. It's nearly impossible to describe with words the truly strange and haunting sound of this work, which is somehow both radically new sounding and oddly nostalgic. The sound of the violin is cracked open and we slither our way inside it, becoming subsumed in its incredible richness. It is almost as if we could take a single lush moment of Mahler or Bruckner and open it up into a whole microuniverse.

Scelsi's idea of looking for a new harmonic dimension inside the sounds — combined with the microlistening and slowly evolving formal processes — was to become a central feature of spectral music. There are many parallels between Scelsi's work and the work of American minimalists, especially Steve Reich, except that the domain of focus was the timbre of a sound for Scelsi and not the rhythmic alignments of the minimalists. Moreover, while Scelsi's music is very process-driven; the processes are not mechanical or automatic but are controlled in a freer, more intuitive manner than is true for the early minimalists.

Scelsi's music, when studied on its own, is often dismissed as fatally limited. Very few of the elements we have come to expect in pieces can be found: almost no melodies, little even in the way of specifically memorable events. The music when listened to inattentively or poorly performed can sometimes sound like little more than a slowly changing drone. When Grisey and Murail combined Scelsi's sometimes naive intuitions with a more in-depth study of acoustics, however, the postelectronic attitude of Ligeti, the artistic integrity and dedication to harmony taught by Messiaen, and their own high levels of compositional "métier,"[19] spectral music was born.

What Shaped the Development of Spectral Music?

Defining a musical movement requires at least some attempt at describing the milieu in which it was shaped. The formation by Tristan Murail of the group L'Itinéraire (especially the performing ensemble that was the public face of the collective) in the early seventies along with the bipolar opposition that existed between the serialist establishment (led by Boulez and his Domaine Musical ensemble) and the spectral young Turks (who, in L'Itinéraire, had their own ensemble) were the cornerstones in the evolution of spectral music.[20]

Trial and Error

A key aspect of early spectral music was its empirical nature. The term "experimental music" generally refers to pieces based directly on untested intellectual speculations,[21] whereas spectral music draws on the concrete results of musical experiments. Especially in the earliest days, the collective L'Itinéraire was a place where a fairly close-knit group of composers and performers (most of the composers were also performing) could try out new ideas, retaining the successes and eliminating the failures. Hugues Dufourt's piece *Saturne,*[22] for example, was created in the aftermath of an enormous phase of experimentation. Dufourt had made reel-to-reel recordings of a vast array of percussion effects. He then used several tape decks to simulate different superpositions from this repertoire. The most striking and successful results of these experiments (read: improvisations) could then be used in the final composition. This sort of experimentation was central to the working method of L'Itinéraire.

Another manifestation of their empiricism was their extensive use of analog electronic instruments. The state of computer technology at the time meant that digital synthesis was an unavoidably slow and cumbersome endeavor. Analog electronic instruments — from the ondes Martenot (a single-line electronic instrument which became popular in the mid-twentieth century) to electric organs to ring modulators — on the other hand, offered a wealth of new resources that could be tested and evaluated. L'Itinéraire had an ensemble of electronic instruments whose members would meet for informal experimental sessions and, in contrast to the traditions of American experimentation and improvisatory performance, these sessions were not the goal, but only a step toward achieving a goal. Just as great improvisers like Bach saw the need to go back to the table and perfect what could be satisfactorily improvised, the composers of L'Itinéraire saw these sessions not as concerts or happenings (they were not public), but as a laboratory in which to test and discover new ideas. These ideas could later be incorporated in the context of fully mastered compositions. This enabled these composers to avoid both the paralysis that can affect a composer who is not constantly searching for new ideas and techniques, and the self-absorption of a composer who realizes his concepts in a pure and untempered form without regard to the musicality or interest of the resulting work.

The early spectral composers, in a curious parallel with some of the early American minimalist composers, were reaping the benefits of being practical music makers in a field full of unheard and sometimes unhearable experiments that were being presented as finished products. This is not to say that the members of L'Itinéraire ceded the intellectual high ground to the serialists who represented the mainstream of new concert music (what the French call "musique savant"). In fact, one of the reasons that L'Intinéraire received government funding in such a relatively short time was that certain other antiBoulez factions (who favored something more like a return to tonality) saw spectral music, which they did not particularly like, as a valuable intellectual counterweight to serialism. At that time, French intellectuals were not disposed to granting force to the populist arguments of the neotonal composers. Of course, those same "conservative" composers who then saw spectral music as an expedient strategic ally now feel free to attack all stripes of "intellectual" music equally. The publications by and about L'Itinéraire are the first forums where the ideas of spectral music were presented to a larger audience.[23] While the importance of this group became less clear in the very late seventies and early eighties — when Grisey moved to America and the ensemble began to function in a more routine manner — its impact on Grisey, Murail, and developing younger composers in the early and mid-seventies was enormous.

The Evil Empire

All revolutions need an enemy, and for spectral musicians the target was clear: serialism. I've been throwing this word around a bit and it's high time I explained it as best I can for nonspecialists.

"Serialism" was originally used to talk about the music written by Arnold Schoenberg and his followers beginning in the early part of the twentieth century. They organized the twelve notes of the chromatic scale into an ordered series. All twelve notes had to be used before any one could be reused; in principle, it was hoped that this would guarantee a sort of equality among the tones, ensuring that the kinds of hierarchy that are so important to tonal music did not creep in. The composer would write a new series — ordering — for each piece and the characteristics of a given order would help determine the character of the work; any order of notes was possible. Using this first version of a given series as a point of departure, the composer could perform permutations of various sorts to generate new variants that they believed would share some structural underpinnings. As serialism developed after World War II in Europe, the use of complete twelve-note series began to disappear and serialism or postserialism came to mean music that used combinatorial procedures for organizing musical parameters (these variants of a given series are called combinatorial permutations by theorists). The idea was that some abstract germ (a set of intervals, or notes, or even just a list of random numbers) could take on myriad musical manifestations, which might seem very different but which — at least metaphysically — ought to have some coherence.

The entrenched position of the well-known serialists was formidable indeed. For most of the public, their music and ideas simply *were* contemporary music. A strong need to rebel against the perceived tyranny of this situation is evident in both the music and articles of the first-generation spectral composers. Where serial pieces of the day were made up of an endless number of pointillistic microevents, spectral pieces contained long stretches of slow evolutions with events occurring only on a large temporal scale. A structural or functional use of harmonic relationships was disdained by twelve-tone composers, but was elevated to a central role in the musical discourse of spectral composers. The advocates of serialism espoused (though rarely actually used) fragmented, nondirectional "panel" and "moment" forms that attempted to create a sequence of "separate" moments or panels that were not intended to "add up" to some larger-scale structure, while the spectralists tried to create process-based evolutionary forms where each event grew out of the previous event. And perhaps most profoundly, the capacities of the music's listeners were no longer something to be mocked (at worst) or elevated through a program of auditory indoctrination in some future, better society (at best). The spectral attitude led these composers to attempt to compose music that could be perceived by any attentive human listener, rather than hoping for some improvement in the society or species whose likelihood is doubtful. They saw the phenomena of auditory perception as a set of fruitful constraints that show what is relevant and what is mere utopian dreaming.[24]

However, as with any bipolar opposition, the differences and the rhetoric were both exaggerated. Even in the earliest spectral pieces, like Grisey's *Partiels*, there are some elements that are organized in a combinatorial manner. Moreover, this opposition that was so central in the 1970s began to weaken in the '80s, when a new generation of less revolutionary spectral composers began to appear. In the '90s (under the common threat of a less intellectual, more "democratic" approach that attacked equally all music that attempted something new — "the people like this so we should give it to them!"), this opposition all but evaporated. The change in attitude can be clearly seen in the contrast between a composer like Murail, who was never involved with serialism, and one like Philippe Hurel,[25] who has always used some combinatorial procedures and who admires that repertoire greatly.

The change from enemy to ally (although this term is perhaps too strong) has not been purely rhetorical or social in nature, but has also manifested itself in the music. Both spectral and postserial music have evolved greatly over the last twenty-five years. Spectral composers no longer disdain all types of contrast or rupture, and few postserialists are now willing to write off the possibilities of human audition as irrelevant to musical composition. Furthermore, a sensitivity to sound seems to have become a ubiquitous requirement for music of any style to be deemed well crafted. As with political movements, both the spectral and serial composers have matured to the point that they can openly acknowledge and influence each other without fear of losing their identity or "polluting" their ideology.

Where Has Spectral Music Gone and Where Is It Going?

Although it may seem strange in a movement that is less than thirty years old, three very distinct groups of composers have emerged that could properly be called "spectral." Most clear is the first generation: Gérard Grisey and Tristan Murail. Together and separately, they helped define the goals and ideals of the movement and have created a legacy of masterpieces that have influenced a broad spectrum of composers. While both have had many students, few of those students have become spectral composers. Both Grisey and Murail adopted Messiaen's approach of encouraging their students to find a personal form of expression (although they certainly have pushed them to give harmony a higher priority than many other composers do).

The second generation of spectral composers (for those who follow new music more closely, I am thinking of composers such as Saariaho, Hurel, Durville, early works by Dalbavie, etc.) all studied with other teachers and initially wrote in more postserial styles. Yet each of these composers was drawn, over time, toward spectral music, and all of them completed brief periods of study (late in their development) with Grisey or Murail. They were drawn to spectral music as an alternative choice, one that would allow them to exploit their particular sensibilities. They are not polemicists by nature and most hold strong sympathies for some other styles of music as well. Although their styles are personal, they do not exhibit the same degree of extreme stylistic rigor that so mark Grisey and Murail, and they often show signs of eclecticism in their works.

In the last ten to fifteen years a third generation of spectral composers, of which I am a part, has begun to emerge (including Jean-Luc
Hervé, François Paris, etc.). This group of composers turned to spectral
music for diverse reasons, but did so much earlier in their development.
All of these composers have studied extensively with Grisey, Murail,
or both. While the languages and aims of these composers are very
different (for example, Paris composes frequently for the voice and is
interested in the lyric possibilities of the spectral language, while my
music is almost exclusively instrumental), they share a greater degree
of ideological fervor than the second generation. This group has delved
deeply into spectral techniques and sought to continue its evolution in
new directions.

Besides individual temperaments, social conditions may explain
some of the difference between the second and third generations.
Whereas the second generation was still in many ways forced to declare
allegiance to a movement, becoming either spectral or remaining postserial, in the still-polarized atmosphere of the time, the composers of
the third generation were free to mix eclectically whatever elements
from whatever styles they chose. Most of Grisey's and Murail's students have, in fact, proceeded in this manner, incorporating elements
of spectral music but not fully embracing the movement. (I do not
count these spectrally influenced composers as belonging to this third
generation.) Those with sympathies for other styles have been free to
pursue these styles, while at the same time integrating some aspects of
spectralism. The real members of this third generation, however, have
forged deeper links with the spectral school. Furthermore, they have
done so without constraint, out of a deep commitment to the spectral
approach. In this way, they more closely resemble the first generation
of spectralists.

So What?

If this attitude I'm describing and this musical lineage I've put forward
really are possible answers to the "how" question, am I predicting they
will somehow "save" new music? While my view is certainly biased,
certain tendencies clearly seem to be forming. The spectral attitude
has already had a major effect on all styles of contemporary European

music. In a historical progression that began in the Baroque period, timbre has moved from an accessory, decorative role to an essential place within the musical discourse. Spectral music has been both the product of this trend and an agent in its recent progress. I think that a musical style that totally ignores "the tones actually sounding" has become an extremely unlikely venture in the twenty-first century. Even the most bloodlessly cerebral of contemporary composers now pay at least lip service to the sonic reality of their music. This achievement is extremely significant and much of the credit belongs to the spectral movement. Composers like Jonathan Harvey and Magnus Lindberg have integrated many elements of spectral music within a decidedly nonspectral language, and this phenomenon seems to be spreading.

During my third year at conservatory, I suddenly felt lost as a composer. I was not sure what to write or why I was writing. I asked myself what had drawn me to music as a child. The answer I finally discovered in myself was the same one Scelsi had found: the sounds. There were sounds I wanted to make and sounds I wanted to hear. No structural principles or intellectual frameworks had motivated my initial love of music, only a sensual fascination with sound. I wanted to compose because there were things I wanted to hear — things that didn't yet exist. We have taken the first steps and made some of the crucial insights; I can't imagine that there will not be future composers who will feel the same need and who will profit from our efforts. They will either build on our work or move in other directions in their search for a personal means of sculpting sound into music.

Moreover, I think that the spectral approach offers the potential for creating really novel musics that are nonetheless perceivable and viscerally satisfying to a wide range of listeners. We should not be surprised that the Impressionists' understanding of light and color led to works that can be appreciated without a great knowledge of iconography and chiaroscuro and ultimately reached a significant and appreciative public. Nor should we be surprised if an approach like that of spectral music turned out to give many new listeners, who possessed an openness to new music and were willing to listen carefully, a way to begin a meaningful relationship with demanding, innovative, even difficult music. In the first part of this book, I pointed out that the decline in the acceptance of new art is due to many aspects of modern society that are essentially independent of considerations of the art itself. But any solution or even improvement of the situation will require both a changed context and fertile ideas ready to bloom in that new context. I don't know if the group of spectral composers has found those ideas, but I know we're out there looking.

Ultimately, what counts is that both sides of the art creator–perceiver contract are fulfilled. You must believe that if you make the effort and sacrifice the time, there will be a reward. Music must not be of interest only to the specialists who make it; it must at least sometimes offer something remarkable and rare to all those who are ready to find it. Music cannot be an affair for the learned specialist; it must be at least potentially accessible to any human being ready to invest the requisite time and effort. Music must be designed not in the abstract as a piece of sonic speculation, but as a work of sound designed to be heard by human beings.

Coda

Endings are hard; any composition teacher will tell you that. You can, of course, fall back on one of the old reliable options:

1. Recapitulation: I could review the main points of the argument and try to tie them into a nice neat bundle that will definitively show my analysis to be definitive.
2. Big, bombastic finale: I could launch into an all-out screed about the things we *must* do if we are to save art for future generations, with an ever-increasing level of rhetorical flourish, leading my readers to give all their money to arts organizations and volunteer every weekend.
3. *Non sequitur* ending: One of my personal favorites — "and now for something completely different" — can create a sensation that is sufficiently unbalanced that everything preceding it is seen in a new light.
4. No-ending ending: I could present some last pearls of analytical insight and then simply stop as if the very lack of conclusion must imply something significant.
5. Fade-out: I could make a last tour of some issues, gradually diminishing the intensity of the rhetoric until the book simply

stops on an ambivalent note (this is the exact inverse of the "Big, bombastic finale").

6. Art-house movie ending: I could sink into despair, overwhelmed by the negative forces arrayed against serious art, until our main character (contemporary classical music) slowly walks out into the onrushing ocean of pop culture to drown.

7. Hollywood ending: I could find some small glimmer of hope and greatly exaggerate its potential for counteracting the trends of the last eighty years. Then I could project that hope forward into a glorious future where high schoolers will fill their iPods with classical works and argue in the hallways about the appropriate tempi for Beethoven symphonies, whether or not Bach ought to be played on a modern piano, and whether microtonality offered more potential for innovation than electroacoustic techniques.

8. Cowardly academic ending: I could simply go on about how impossible it is to predict how things might develop going forward.

9. Cliff-hanger: I could end with a whole series of questions and unknowns about the future, without putting forward an image of how things might turn out in the end.

Even if I really wanted to, it's probably impossible to completely avoid all of these formulas. More important, why *would* I want to? Many of these schemas yield satisfying endings. That's how they became old reliables: They work. However, the desire for a satisfying form can put pressure on the still inchoate content and turn it into little more than a hackneyed cliché. You can think of all those movies where you know exactly what will happen during the last ten minutes when there are still more than twenty minutes to go. This kind of ending can offer a satisfying effect of ritual closure, but it rarely adds anything of much value to what has already transpired.

I think the best course of action for me might be to create a hybrid ending. Let's start with a *non sequitur*. I had a concert in October 2004 where two pieces were to be played and then recorded on successive days in the same hall. The concert went fine, but as we were setting up for the recording, we noticed a low frequency hum in the hall (it was too soft to hear in a full hall, but much too loud for a recording). We tried the usual solutions of turning off electrical devices and the heating system blowers, but the noise would not go away. The director of the theater even brought in a technician from their HVAC company to try to identify and eliminate the noise, but to no avail. It seems the noise was either caused by the air circulation system of an underground parking garage next door, which could not be deactivated without giving carbon monoxide poisoning to the attendants, or by the vibrations transmitted from a nearby highway, which apparently could not be diverted just for us. In and of itself, this is the sort of annoying contretemps requiring frenzied phone calls and called-in favors that everyone faces occasionally, and it is not very illuminating. What struck me as unusual and fairly encouraging was the response of the other institutions we contacted in an effort to come up with a plan B.

New music CDs are made on budgets flimsier than shoestrings, so renting commercial studio time was not an option. In France, where these concerts were held and where this ensemble is based, the normal solution is to line up a long list of publicly supported institutions and studios as "coproducers" who contribute free studio time on the days that they have no paying work. This works out for them because they can list the coproduction in their year-end reports and make it seem as though they are doing a lot with their subsidy, without spending much extra. This has often meant choosing alliances carefully, however, because each institution understandably wants to project the sense that it is essential and unique. Therefore, asking one studio for help often meant foreclosing the possibility of using some other studio. When we started calling around for help, however, this was not the reaction we got. Instead of people saying, "Well, you're in with so and so, why not ask them?" we found an immediate willingness to help (as long as it did not engender any direct costs for them). Within a few hours we had two or three different possibilities lined up. Now this might not sound like very much, but it is.

As support for culture in France (where I was living at the time) began its steep decline beginning in the mid-1990s, the first reaction was not the sort of unified action one might have hoped for. Rather, each composer, ensemble, and institution struggled ever harder to hold onto his or her piece of an ever-smaller pie. We were all complicit in this. Even some groups that had diminished in quality would receive all the composers' support in maintaining their subsidy, because we knew that money taken from one place would never be reallocated in another: It would simply vanish into the ether. Each group of composers became more and more partisan, publishers practically stopped signing new composers, and so on. And this wasn't unique to France. In the days following 9/11, when many of the New York–based foundations rightly felt obligated to redirect much of their funding from arts to more basic health and welfare projects, the same reaction among the composers and ensembles ensued.

Musical composition (and perhaps any life as an artist) is a deeply self-centered existence. We work most of the time alone in a room trying to hone an ever more personal vision. We come into contact with the outside world only much later and in fleeting bursts. Under normal circumstances, we do not and probably should not think much about the rest of society. The current position of art in society, however, could hardly be described as normal compared to 50, 100, or 150 years ago.

Despite the pressures all arts groups and artists are feeling, though, there are rays of hope, such as the group of studios who offered to help out when I was faced with my emergency back in 2004. The point of my story is this: I believe that the real peril and perhaps real possibility of the current situation is finally sinking in.

I actually believe that we are at something of a critical juncture, a tipping point. Composers no longer have the clout with politicians or the public to impose their will (as they did in the immediate post–World War II era). If difficult, demanding art that requires large-scale subsidies is to continue, it will only be with society's consent. If we artists are unable or unwilling to make the case, we will quickly find ourselves in the position of the Komodo dragon, living on one small island and in a few zoos as we watch our population wither away and our habitat shrink to oblivion. While my generation can probably go on eking out some sort of continuation for ourselves, there can be no guarantee of a future for this kind of nonfunctional, non-cost-effective art if we don't make one. While decades ago it might have seemed sufficient to gripe about inadequate rehearsal time for difficult pieces, now that just won't work. We need to convince the players to do more, work for free, raise extra funds, or do whatever it takes. We can't offer mediocre performances of mediocre works and hope that systemic inertia will be enough to preserve the status quo. Not making people walk out is not an achievement.

It is very likely that the generations alive today will either see nonfunctional subsidized art begin to reestablish a societal consensus about the value and importance of its existence, or watch it dwindle into a marginal existence while waiting for the last of us to die off. This latter outcome seems to me so unacceptable that I am unwilling to just sit back and watch it happen (after all, I probably already have my sinecure in the Komodo dragon's nature preserve locked up). And while part of me believes that the best way to fight this is through great art, another part thinks that great art can only shape culture if someone is listening or looking. If I can't convince you of even the potential importance of difficult, nonfunctional art, how can I expect you to support it passively with your acceptance, much less to support it actively with your time, attention, and perhaps even money?

When I was living and working solely as a composer, I didn't think much about these issues because everyone I came into contact with "got it." But since I began teaching nonspecialists regularly in the late 1990s, I realized how great the peril really is. So much of the value system I had always assumed was a shared part of Western culture is no longer universal (if it ever really was). And no matter how good our marketing and promotion savvy becomes, or how hard we try, I don't believe we will ever come up with a way of justifying the existence of this sort of art through personal taste or market preferences alone. Moreover, the simple call for diversity as an absolute good won't help either, because one kind of diversity is as good as another and may be much cheaper or more popular to boot.

I'd been thinking about a new way of restating the importance of this "useless" art when I attended a lecture/debate between the humanist, Louis Menand, and the evolutionary psychologist and linguist, Steven Pinker. Pinker discussed a study of perceived facial beauty. Apparently this study showed that a composite image created by averaging together all the faces in a group (this averaging is done feature by feature: average lip thickness, average distance between the eyes, average height of the forehead, etc.) is universally judged more attractive than any of the individuals in the group that went into the averaged composite. This scientist responsible for this work had stumbled on his results by chance when trying to come up with the composite face of a group of criminals. He had thought to produce the epitome of a criminal face and instead ended up with what he judged to be a pretty handsome man. Through a series of experiments, he was surprised to find that this works with any group. Our sense of beauty is somehow (even the scientist doing the work was not proposing exactly how) influenced by all the faces that we have seen — whether we find them beautiful, ugly, or indifferent. At dinner after the talk, Pinker amplified this point, saying that this research suggests that even a racist's idea of facial beauty will become more multicultural as the population he encounters and the images he sees vary: It is affected only by the faces he or she sees, not what he might think about those faces. There is no sense in which this process is directly influenced by personal taste; rather, taste is influenced by this process. Pinker pointed out that post hoc studies of the face types chosen by advertisers underline this idea. The models used to represent beauty in America in the more homogeneous 1950s were in the Doris Day mold, while now advertisers are more likely to choose someone like Halle Berry. The humanist, Menand was deeply skeptical and felt that, even if true, this finding was not of interest: "science cares about the means" he said, while arguing that the humanities is more interested in the outliers.

On some level, I think both of them were partially incorrect. The real question we need to worry about (unless, I suppose, we work in advertising or sales) is not what face or song or picture packs the most wallop in an instantaneous rating of attractiveness, beauty, or memorability. The kind of art that we've been discussing is deeply ill-suited to one-night stands and instant gratification. The deeper implication of the study on facial beauty is that only by seeing things that we do not immediately find the "most beautiful" can our notion of beauty develop; whether the mechanism of this development turns out to be a mechanical calculation of means, or something more subtle, is secondary. If, in some way, what we find beautiful is the sum (or, more precisely, the average) of all the things we see, then we ought to be very sure that we don't just keep fixating on our current notion of beauty. We could think of art as pure research into the potential beauty or ugliness of some superficially unpromising avenues. To paraphrase Gérard Grisey, art is much more about becoming than being, and this is, I think, the real lesson of that study on beauty.

I'd like to put this into a context: One of the classes I sometimes teach is a seminar on composition for undergraduates. In this class each student works on a piece over the course of the semester. I try very hard not to push them in any particular aesthetic direction and often the works they write sound more like Mozart than like modern pieces. Most of these students merely want to try their hand at writing something; the majority have no ambitions of becoming professional or even serious amateur composers. While I don't try to make them write "modern-sounding" music, I do make them listen to a lot of different music.

One of the composers we invariably deal with is Iannis Xenakis (1922–2001). Xenakis was a Greek-born composer who spent most of his career in Paris. He used the mathematical and architectural training he had received to bring a highly idiosyncratic approach to composition. His works began life more often as graphical drawings or mathematical formalizations than as themes or motives. At first listen, many of his works have little in common with what these students think of as "music." The sounds can be loud and grating; there are slow changes, but little that is recognizable within traditional categories of melody, harmony, and rhythm. Yet once the students get over their shock, they never feel that there is nothing there. Clearly, shape, movement, intent, form, and, in the best of his works, an amazing raw power can be detected. When we've listened to and discussed all of this at some length from a purely descriptive point of view, someone will invariably venture: But is it music? At this point, I generally get the real rush of hearing the students argue among themselves about the effectiveness or memorability of these sorts of mass-based sonic constructions. Someone often raises a question about the composer's obligation to attach his or her music to a tradition. The idea of expressing abstract platonic forms within the sonic medium is also a perennial topic. In the end, however, the conclusion is almost always that there is a real musical intent, regardless of what tools were used to produce that result. I'm sure many of the students go away believing that it is not very good music, but they can all hear the echo of a composer's will in the sounds. It is not noise, and it is not random. By hearing these works, their notions of music and beauty are altered forever; the mean of the bell curve in their mind has been shifted at least a little bit.

You could say that anything will shift this mean, but I don't think that just anything will be effective. For those beauty experiments, the image must be recognizably a face and it ought to be different in some way from other faces if the change is going to have much of an impact. Moreover, it ought to be the kind of difference that you want to look at enough for it to really burn into your senses and leave a lasting impression. And this is precisely what abstract, difficult, sometimes overly intellectual art that attaches itself to a tradition while frequently negating almost every aspect of that tradition, that still believes in criteria of worth and the relationship between a creator and a created object, tries to do (successfully or not). That many things, even many strange things, can be wonderful art doesn't mean that everything can or will be wonderful art. The choice often seems to be posed today as if we must either take it all or leave it completely — but this is absurd. What we must do is consent to and perhaps even support its existence, if we still want to be able to make choices about what to accept or reject in the future.

A real danger exists that, as marketing and focus groups learn to locate our current preferences with ever greater precision, the range of stimuli we receive will draw ever tighter. If we only go to a museum to see over and over again the paintings we already love, we are not developing into anything: We are like rats in a cage pulling the lever that will deliver us a reward until we get so sated we fall asleep. Moreover, the jolt we get each time is less fulfilling than the last. The malaise of the modern condition often feels like we've already "been there, done that." But there are so many things we have not seen or heard — an essentially endless supply. Yet we must put up with the discomfiture of travel if we are to discover a new place, if we are to return home with slightly different eyes. If the orchestra only plays what we already know we want to hear, we will never hear anything new and we will never find a new way to hear the pieces we already love. It may be reassuring, it may be entertaining, but it is not enough, or at least I hope not.

One final *non sequitur*: There have been many recent articles about the wonderful new addition to the Museum of Modern Art in New York. Almost all offer this as a sign of the great health in modern visual arts. Yet what gets mentioned only in passing is the great tragedy of this institution's meaning for art. MoMA was founded to keep only works less than fifty years old. The idea was that older works, once sorted, would move on to real museums, while MoMA was about creation. Now, of course, they could never do that: Those "brand name" paintings are what pull people in and allow the museum to charge the very high admission fee needed to support the institution. MoMA now thinks of itself as a museum of twentieth-century art or perhaps a museum of Modernist art. There is nothing wrong with this, except that it is the kind of idealism that created the original MoMA (with its time limit on paintings' chance to prove themselves) that leads to remarkable art. The sort of savvy management and marketing combined with scholarship and respect that created the current MoMA can create institutions, not inspire art. It seems to me the original mission — even if it meant small shows in patrons' apartments — was much more ambitious and admirable than the new $400-million-dollar MoMA with its role as theme park for the culturally savvy and well heeled.

I don't want to waste too much time on recapitulation or in an effort to tie things into a too neat a bundle. Ultimately, it is not for me to decide what will happen; I don't think I even wrote this book with much of a realistic hope of convincing you of my position (though I certainly hope that I've achieved this mission). The real reason that I've spent so much time on this is that I think, whether it wants to or not, society is currently in the process of choosing — through action or inaction — whether nonpopular, nonfunctional art will remain a viable part of our culture, or become a historical topic that scholars in two hundred years will look back upon as a sort of aberration, a hopeless romantic gesture. So few of the people I meet seem to grasp that the choice is in our hands only if we face the problem and do not let the choice be made without any conscious intervention, debate, or even regret.

Let me be clear: I am not saying music will disappear, or storytelling, drawing, painting, or sculpture. I am saying that this relatively recent, relatively fragile tradition of functionless, complex art, which has produced such strange and remarkable results, is at risk. The infrastructure it requires is so massive and so expensive; the demands it places on time, training, resources, and attention are absurdly high. If we (both artists and public) continue to view an ever-increasing marginalization of this art with acceptance, this kind of art will become nothing but a strange curiosity. I can see the future students now gasping in wonder at the idea of people going to so much trouble to read *Finnegan's Wake.*

The moment I would like you to focus on is not the initial shock of strangeness when you first come across something really new and perhaps even a little odd. Rather, it is the moment that very rarely, but sometimes, happens two or three years later when you come across the same work again: All sense of strangeness is gone and you just gape at the beauty. You can't understand what could have seemed so strange or even so difficult in the first place. Exorbitant luxury that those handful of moments in a lifetime are, I'd hate to see us decide they were no longer worth the price.

So the next time you're introduced to a composer at a cocktail party, may I suggest the following:

"So, you're a composer? [no guffaw, but perhaps just a touch of curiosity or pleasant surprise] Is there any way I might hear some of your music?"

That's the only question that really matters in the end.

Notes

Chapter 1

1. Alice Goldfarb Marquis, *Art Lessons: Learning from the Rise and Fall of Public Funding* (New York: Basic Books, 1995), 258.
2. Nicholas Humphrey, *Leaps of Faith* (New York, Basic Books, 1996).
3. Jürgen Habermas, "Modernity — An Incomplete Project," in *The Anti-Aesthetic: Essays on Postmodern Culture*, ed. Hal Foster (Port Townsend, Washington: Bay Press, 1983).
4. Thomas Kuhn, *The Structure of Scientific Revolutions* (Cambridge, MA: MIT Press, 1962).
5. Alvin H. Reiss, Don't Just Applaud — Send Money!: The Most Successful Strategies for Funding and Marketing the Arts (New York: Theatre Communications Group, Inc., 1995).
6. Alice Goldfarb Marquis, *Art Lessons: Learning from the Rise and Fall of Public Funding* (New York: Basic Books 1995), 249.
7. Jean Galard, "Une question capitale pour l'esthétique," in *Qu'est-ce qu'un chef-d'oeuvre?* (Paris: Musée du Louvre/Editions Gallimard, 2000).
8. MacGregor, Neil, "Chef-d'oeuvre — valeur sûre?" in *Qu'est-ce qu'un chef-d'oeuvre?* (Paris: Musée du Louvre/Editions Gallimard, 2000).
9. Alice Goldfarb Marquis, *Art Lessons: Learning from the Rise and Fall of Public Funding* (New York: Basic Books 1995), 102.
10. Research and Forecasts, "The Importance of the Arts and Humanities to American Society" (Washington, D.C.: National Cultural Alliance, 1993).
11. Joseph Rody in W. MacNeil Lowry, ed., *Performing Arts and American Society* (Englewood Cliffs, N.J.: Prentice-Hall), 1978.

12. Some more extreme interpretations of quantum dynamics might suggest a more privileged role for knowing and observing, but I'm going to leave those very complex and not widely accepted ideas out of the current discussion.

13. Harold Bloom, *The Western Canon: The Books and School of the Ages* (New York: Riverhead Books, 1994), 17.

14. In Chapter 7, I will offer some hypothetical candidates for universals that might relate to music.

Chapter 2

1. Herbert J. Gans, *Popular Culture and High Culture* (New York, Basic Books, 1999).

2. Henry James, preface to *The Wings of the Dove* (New York: Modern Library, 1930), xxvii–xxviii.

3. G. A. Miller, "The Magical Number Seven, Plus or Minus Two: Some Limits on Our Capacity for Processing Information," *The Psychological Review*, vol. 63 (1956): 81–97.

Chapter 3

1. Excerpt from "Entretien avec Daniel Buren: L'art n'est plus justifiable ou les pointes sur les 'I,'" translated by Alexander Alberro and reprinted in Alexander Alberro and Blake Stimson, eds., *Conceptual Art: A Critical Anthology* (Cambridge, MA: MIT Press. 1999), 69.

2. First published in the catalogue for the exposition "January 5–31, 1969," New York: Seth Siegelaub, 1969 and reprinted in Alexander Alberro and Blake Stimson, eds., *Conceptual Art: A Critical Anthology* (Cambridge, MA: MIT Press, 1999), xxii.

3. First published in Willoughby Sharp, "Lawrence Weiner at Amsterdam," *Avalanche* 4 (Spring 1972): 66, 69, 70; reprinted in Alexander Alberro and Blake Stimson, eds., *Conceptual Art: A Critical Anthology* (Cambridge, MA: MIT Press. 1999), xxxii–xxxiii.

4. Sarah Charlesworth, "A Declaration of Dependence," in Alexander Alberro and Blake Stimson, eds., *Conceptual Art: A Critical Anthology* (Cambridge, MA: MIT Press, 1999), 314.

5. Wallace Stevens, "The Relations between Poetry and Painting," undated pamphlet published by the Museum of Modern Art and reprinted in Arthur Berger's *Reflections of an American Composer* (Berkeley: University of California Press, 2002), 51.

6. This overview of the history of the chef-d'oeuvre draws heavily on Matthias Waschek's "Le chef-d'oeuvre: un fait culturel," in *Qu'est-ce qu'un chef-d'oeuvre?* (Paris: Musée du Louvre/Editions Gallimard), 2000.

Chapter 4

1. William A. Henry, *In Defense of Elitism* (New York: Doubleday, 1994), 2–3.

2. Gaetano Mosca, in *The Ruling Class*, trans. Hannah D. Kahn, ed. Arthur Livingston, as reprinted in Harry K. Girvetz, ed., *Democracy and Elitism* (New York: Charles Scribner's Sons, 1967), 280–81.

Chapter 5

1. Glorianna Davenport, "Your Own Virtual Storyworld," *Scientific American* (November 2000): 80.

2. It would not be appropriate to go into a lengthy discussion of temperaments here, but for those unfamiliar with the notion, a brief elaboration is required. Since at least the time of the Greeks, musicians and theorists have realized that there is no perfect way to tune an instrument. The main musical intervals are formed by creating simple ratios between the fundamental frequencies (or equivalently by dividing strings into simple fractions). For example, an octave is created by doubling the frequency or halving the string length. When you try to create a full scale this way, it doesn't work, however. The ratio for a perfect fifth is 3:2, and while it is possible to generate all twelve notes of the chromatic scale by cycling up through eleven successive fifths, when you finally get back to what should be the same pitch as your starting note (though seven octaves higher) with a twelfth perfect fifth, you will find that the note is significantly higher than it should be. In other words, it does not form an octave relation with the note that you started on. The distance between where this note ends up and where it should end up is called the Comma of Pythagoras. [For those who want to check the math 3/2 to the twelfth power gives you a note at 129.746 times your starting frequency, whereas the actual note seven octaves up should be 2 to the seventh power (or 128) times the starting frequency.] Temperaments are basically the art of hiding this comma, either by making a few intervals very out of tune while the rest are reasonably close to their theoretically "perfect" values or by making many intervals slightly out of tune. There

is, unfortunately, no way to make everything in tune with everything else; the math just doesn't work.

3. A "perfectly" in-tune third has a frequency ratio of 4:3 between the fundamental frequencies of the two notes.

4. "Peter Weibel: Ars Electronica: An Interview by Johan Pijnappel," *Art & Design Profile No. 39 Art and Technology* (London: Academy Group Ltd., 1994), 29.

5. I am using the term "computer music" here to refer very broadly to music written to be "performed" with electronic apparatuses and computer programs. Much of this music is "performed" directly by the composer in a studio and comes to the audience in prerecorded form. Live electronic traditions also exist, however, as does hybrid mixed music that marries acoustic instruments and electronic sounds, treatments, or processes.

Chapter 6

1. L. Henry Schaffer, "How to Interpret Music," in Mari Riess Jones and Susan Holleran, eds., *Cognitive Bases of Musical Communication* (Washington, D.C.: American Psychological Association, 1992), 263.

2. Steven Pinker, *The Language Instinct: How the Mind Creates Language* (New York: W. Morrow and Co., 1994), 237.

3. Ibid., 238.

4. George Miller wrote a famous article discussing the importance of units consisting of five to nine elements: G. A. Miller (1956), "The magical number seven, plus or minus two: Some limits on our capacity for processing information," *Psychological Review* 63: 81–97.

5. Sandra E. Trehub; E. Glenn Schellenberg; Stuart B. Kamenetsky, "Infants' and adults' perception of scale structure," *Journal of Experimental Psychology: Human Perception & Performance*, Vol. 25(4) (Aug. 1999): 965–75.

6. Carol Krumhansl, *Cognitive Foundations of Musical Pitch* (New York: Oxford University Press, 1990).

7. "Learning and Perceiving Musical Structures: Further Insights from Artificial Neural Networks," Barbara Tillman; Jamshed J. Bharucha; Emmanuel Bigand; in *Cognitive Neuroscience of Music*, Isabelle Peretz, Dept. of Psychology, University of Montreal (London: Oxford University Press, 2003), 109–23.

8. This idea was first suggested to me by Joseph Dubiel.

9. One can find reasonably successful composers working today who use random or semirandom permutations of a small set of numbers as the

basis for their music. They then map the lists of numbers generated by their permutations to musical parameters to generate their scores. In fairness, this mapping often leaves them room to use their ears and turn the music into something worthwhile, but it remains mystifying to me what benefit they think could flow from a list of arbitrarily permutated signs and symbols.

Chapter 7

1. *La Sonate. Etude de son évolution technique historique et expressive en vue de l'interprétation et de l'audition*, (Paris: Ed. Rouart, Lerolle et Cie, 1913).

Chapter 8

1. It is, of course, possible that we are not "hard-wired" with these intuitions, but, rather, that they are learned through our constant exposure to natural sounds that have simple acoustic structures (harmonic overtones, amplitude modulations, source-filter relations, etc.). Because this exposure has been shown to begin in utero, however, and because we cannot change the basic nature of oscillatory vibrations in the natural world, they might as well be "built-in."

2. I will be drawing many of these examples from an appendix I wrote for a volume of the *Contemporary Music Review*, Vol. 19 (2) 2001.

3. Dufourt's use of the term was in an early article ("Musique spectrale," Paris, Société Nationale de Radiodiffusion, Radio France/Société Internationale de Musique Contemporaine [SIMC], 1979 III, 30–32.) when the spectral movement was still coalescing and was not accompanied by any sort of definition that would be useful in the current context.

4. Many recent electronic sounds have less of this "artificial" quality. This is not due to any real technological progress in generating appropriate complexity; it is because most of these sounds contain information captured from acoustic sounds that have been modified. We still have great difficulty modeling all of these fluctuations.

5. Personal communication.

6. This analysis and, in fact, the sound analyzed are not identical to those used by Grisey when he wrote the piece in the early 1970s (although I have tried to mimic Grisey's procedures as much as possible), and thus there are several differences in the details of the realization. For example, the loudest partial in Grisey's realization is the fifth, whereas in mine it is the ninth. (This is probably due to the sound I analyzed

being performed more loudly than the one used by Grisey; with brass the louder the note is played, generally the higher in the overtone series the loudest partials will be. This is what creates the "brassy" sound.) Another important difference is that the low double bass, which seems to be presenting the fundamental along with the trombone is, in fact, an octave too low. This note is in that octave for separate formal and gestural reasons, however. This note's separation from the other pitches of the instrumental synthesis is reflected in its exclusion from the composer's annotations of partial rankings for each of the other pitches.

7. J. Fineberg, "Appendix II — Musical Examples," *Contemporary Music Review* 19 (2) 2001.

8. I use the metaphor of sculpting in time to evoke the compositional process of a spectral composer who highlights certain groups of frequencies and eliminates others — as a sculptor does with stone — in an effort to create a sonic entity, in time, whose shape and movement corresponds to the composer's intent.

9. In France an academic is a member of the academy, not a university professor (the term for that is an "universitaire"). Thus, by academicism the French mean an officially sanctioned (and often uninspired) musical style and not a pejoratively scholastic one as we would mean by the term in America.

10. The Italian futurist movement began around 1909 and was dedicated to using technology and moving away from gracefulness and craft to the brute force of our industrial future. In this context, however, their link to the spectralists was a desire to make music with sounds not normally believed to be musical. This led to quite a bit of sonic exploration.

11. More generally, it is difficult to imagine spectral music having developed without the arrival of analog electronic music. From the sonic objects of "musique concrète" to the real-time treatments of ring-modulators, the works of early electronic music offered an invaluable stock of models to the later works of spectral composers.

12. The summer courses at Darmstadt became, in the years after World War II, a sort of Mecca for young serial composers. They heard performances, made connections, and spread ideas. The journal they published out of these meetings became a bible for European serial and postserial composers. The hallmark of serial technique is that it attempts and to a great degree succeeds in making all pitches equally important. This is in contrast to the "tonal" system, where notes are organized hierarchically in keys. The problem is that harmonic sensations like tension and release or departure and return can become nearly impossible when all pitches

have equal weight. In music theoretical terms, serialism creates flat pitch spaces in which there are few if any landmarks.

13. Tristan Murail, "L'exigence vis-à-vis de l'acte artistique," *Le Monde de la Musique* 156 (June 1992).

14. Tristan Murail in *Olivier Messiaen*, Harry Halbreich, Fayard/SACEM, 1980.

15. In recent years he has basically acknowledged this, saying that were he younger and more energetic, that is where he would explore. Yet Ligeti is not and never really was a good candidate to perform any sort of slow and meticulous development of a style. He has always been a stylistic experimenter (in the best sense), coming up with an idea, exploring some of its potential, and then moving on.

16. By the late seventies, there was no longer a French Rome Prize that bore the name. The award that is so well known through Berlioz's *Memoires* was scaled down and became the award of a "sejour" at the Villa Médicis in Rome. In many ways, this was still the same award — two years in Rome, concerts, a stipend, and some money to travel; however, the official title of an award winner is a "pensionnaire à la Villa Medicis." Since the English-speaking world still thinks of this award as the Rome Prize — and the American version still bears that name — I have referred to it as such.

17. Murail spoke about the relationship between the composers of L'Itinéraire (himself, Grisey, and Lévinas, in particular) and Scelsi in a conference given in 1987 in Royaumont during their "Voix Nouvelles 87" festival. This conference was transcribed by Marc Texier and published as "Scelsi, L'Itinéraire – L'exploration du son," in *Le Journal à Royaumont* 2 (February 1988).

18. Quoted in the liner notes for the CD Giacinto Scelsi, Accord 200612, 1989.

19. By "microlistening," I mean an extremely close listening where small fluctuations like slight crescendos or tiny glissandi can become major events.

20. The French term *métier* is very difficult to translate; the closest approximation in English is "craft." It implies the full range of techniques and skills required by a profession.

21. The current situation is quite different: The group L'Itinéraire has become something else under other leadership, and the serial-spectral tensions which began to ease in the early eighties — through an IRCAM sponsored effort to promote détente — have by now largely

disappeared. These factors were of critical importance in the seventies when spectral music was first coming into being, however.

22. In the period between the end of World War II and the 1970s all sorts of musical experiments were tried, from using mathematical mapping and statistical distributions to algorithmically "write" pieces, to using the *I Ching* or random number generators to decide on the contents of a work. Other ideas included multiday performances of a single chord, or pieces written for radios where the results will depend on what is on the airwaves during the performance. Some pieces were even literally conceptual and could not be performed, except as a sort of thought experiment.

23. Hugues Dufourt is not really a spectral composer, for me; although his music does explore a fascinating array of sonic colors and combinations, its organization is combinatorial in nature and not sonic. He was, however, a fellow traveler with Grisey and Murail, and this experience is indicative of the spirit of the group and the time.

24. One point of clarification needs to be offered as to the nonsynonymous relation between the composers who belonged to L'Itinéraire and spectral composers. Although at the beginning they all shared many of the same ideas and interests, they gradually evolved in very different directions. Grisey and Murail became the first full-fledged spectral composers, while the others moved in various directions, some being reabsorbed into the larger contemporary music population and others following a more solitary route. As with evolutionary speciation, it is difficult to define the exact moment when the spectral movement became a definite tendency and not part of the broader spectrum of ideas circulating in this group; nonetheless, in hindsight one can see the formation of gradually widening rifts within the collective and at some point the ideas of spectral music can clearly be seen to exist independently from other types of preoccupations that had interested the group.

25. This is not to suggest that musical training is not valuable — in particular auditory training. I am deeply skeptical, however, of there again being a sufficiently homogenous musical common practice to allow the kind of overlearned schemata that effect our perception of tonal music to be developed for contemporary styles. Furthermore, I believe that many of the auditory demands made by serialists of this era exceed the capacity of the human auditory apparatus, regardless of training.

26. Don't worry if you've never heard of many of the composers I mention: I am including them to give some extra context to those familiar with their work, but the argument should still make sense to other readers who just skip over the names.

Index

157